PANTS
ON
FIRE

Cutting through the Biggest Lies
of Twenty-first-Century American Plutocracy

PAUL CHRISTOPHERSON

iUniverse, Inc.
New York   Bloomington

Pants on Fire
Cutting through the Biggest Lies of Twenty-first-Century American Plutocracy

iUniverse books may be ordered through booksellers or by contacting:

iUniverse
1663 Liberty Drive
Bloomington, IN 47403
www.iuniverse.com
1-800-Authors (1-800-288-4677)

Because of the dynamic nature of the Internet, any Web addresses or links contained in this book may have changed since publication and may no longer be valid. The views expressed in this work are solely those of the author and do not necessarily reflect the views of the publisher, and the publisher hereby disclaims any responsibility for them.

ISBN: 978-1-4502-3772-7 (sc)
ISBN: 978-1-4502-3773-4 (dj)
ISBN: 978-1-4502-3774-1 (ebk)

Library of Congress Control Number: 2010909471

Printed in the United States of America

iUniverse rev. date: 08/04/2010

PANTS ON FIRE

Belief in truth begins with doubting all that has hitherto been believed to be true.

Friedrich Nietzsche,
1844—1900

A man's most valuable trait is a judicious sense of what not to believe.

Euripides,
485—406 B.C.

Wherever men hold unequal power in society, they will strive to maintain it. They will use whatever means are most convenient to that end, and will seek to justify them by the most plausible arguments they are able to devise.

Reinhold Niebuhr, 1932
Moral Man and Immoral Society, chapter 2

Contents

INTRODUCTION

This book is about lies. It is about the lies that govern our lives in twenty-first-century America. It is about how they prevail, not on the merits, but by force. It is about all of us who go along with them and what it costs us to do so. It is about who benefits and who pays for it. It is about what needs to happen for us to come to our senses.

The thesis of this book is that a plutocracy has taken over our lives. It has replaced democracy. It demands and gets what it wants from the system—it has become the system—at huge cost to the rest of us. This is what we are all so angry about, and should be—all of us who are not in on the grab.

After this Introduction, I will make no further mention of the war in Iraq, because that is not the subject of this book. But we need to here, since no discussion of lying would be complete without it, and its absence would only reveal a regrettable timidity on our part. Also, it may illustrate the theme—namely, American life

1

organized around a lie, a whole society's behavior patterned by it. The Iraq war is just an example here; this book is about others.

I am talking here about what Joe Conason in his book calls "Big Lies", except maybe bigger. The lies that control a whole modern society and force it to do things that are plainly wrong, not in hindsight, but at the time. The war in Iraq was a natural consequence of the culture of lying. It is a treasure trove of hallmarks of that culture, a big illustration of our society as liars and compliers.

This definition leaves out, as will this book, the lies that are basically private and personal. That is not to condone them— lying is lying. It is just to say that your or my nonviolent sexual escapades or tendencies, and the lies we tell about them, are not likely to exert undue influence on millions of people. Fascination with them springs more from a petty desire to be salacious than from a sincere concern for the public welfare.

The big lie about Iraq was not the one about weapons of mass destruction, which got way too much attention and could too easily be defended. Instead, it was a whole set of lies that grew up around 9/11:

- 9/11 could not have been anticipated or prevented;
- a military war is the way to fight terrorism, even though the whole point of terrorism is that it cannot be fought militarily;

- we cannot catch Osama because he is in the mountains, and anyway he has been "marginalized";
- Iraq and Saddam were involved in 9/11.

That last one was particularly deadly; it has gotten almost 4,400 Americans killed so far, plus God knows how many innocent Iraqis. Some of us knew, and wrote, in June of 2002, that there was no such connection, that the very nature of Saddam's Iraq was that if there was any terrorism to be done, he would do it, not al Qaeda or anybody else; that there would be no affiliations.

But a year later tens of thousands of Americans, believing they were hitting back for those killed on 9/11, found themselves on troop ships headed for Iraq. And even a year after that, in the summer of 2004, 70 percent of America still believed that Iraq was involved in 9/11. They did not come to this by sitting at home looking out the living room window; they had a lot of help arriving at this conclusion.

In fact, as recently as 2008, we could still hear statements like, "We are in Iraq fighting the same enemy that attacked us on 9/11," or, "Since we have been in Iraq we have not been attacked again," or, "The world is better off," or, "The only way to fail is to leave."

Finally, in March 2007, the Pentagon inspector general issued a 121-page report saying that the assertions of a Saddam/al Qaeda link "undercut" the views of the intelligence community, which is government double-talk meaning that the claims were not faulty intelligence but lies. The report called the Defense Department analysis "inappropriate", like putting your feet up on the coffee table or not curbing your dog.

My point is not to be argumentative or disagreeable about the war in Iraq. America has decided to walk away from the obvious treason that that war was, so now it is just tedious to mention it. It does, however, bring out several characteristics of mass control by lying.

First, the manipulator class is populated with very smart people. Their arguments may be sophistry, but it is remarkably clever sophistry. Second, an assertion made forcefully enough can have an effect even greater than if it were true. The manipulators include some very forceful people—people who are accustomed to getting their way and who know how to get it. Forcefulness can be extended to include name-calling, shouting, and intimidation, although these may be carried out by willing supporters.

Instead of discussing the issue calmly in Aristotelian fashion, just find a pejorative label to apply to the dissenter, and the argument is won. This technique does not need to be responsibly applied. Thus a "socialist", according to *Webster's*, is someone who advocates government ownership of the means of production and no private property, but a person need not have advocated any such thing to be called a socialist.

A third technique for getting your way is to fund think tanks and then commission them to do studies supportive of your point of view. One of the more remarkable of these studies came out in late 2006, and it concluded that the U.S. forces serving in Iraq constitute a cross-section of America, representative of all different groups. The point of this study was to portray Americans' commitment as inclusive, democratic, a sort of Athens v. Sparta, when everyone knew who really was and was not doing the fighting and dying.

I found this last instance particularly offensive. It shows the lengths to which the manipulators will go. I have read for the past seven years the names, branch, rank, and hometown of all the names of those killed in Iraq. I have watched for hometowns like the ones listed below.

Chevy Chase, MD   Wellesley, MA
Shaker Heights, OH   Wayzata, MN
Greenwich, CT   Winnetka, IL
Bedford, NY   Short Hills, NJ
Radnor, PA   Ladue, MO
River Oaks, TX   Buckhead, GA
Grosse Point, MI

To my knowledge, none of the dead, out of almost 4,400, came from any of these towns or towns like them. People from these towns experienced the war as a series of tax cuts. For the authors of this study to have asserted the cross-section thesis was contemptible. Since people are not normally that bad, it is reasonable to assume the authors had been bought.

Another Iraq war lie was the one about supporting the troops. The continuous stream of "supplementals" was pitched as being support for the troops. In the spring of 2007, there was another supplemental, this time for $124 billion. This came to $855,000 per troop then in Iraq, or enough to buy each troop ten S-class Mercedes. Obviously, this was not support for the troops, although we will never know where all the money did go. In the fall of 2007, there was a $200 billion supplemental, which could have been paid as bonuses of $1.25 million per troop in Iraq.

This illustrates one final technique—calling something indefensible by a high-sounding name. The most memorable example of this occurred several years ago. It was a tax giveaway to multinationals called the Jobs Creation Act, a forgiveness of taxes on repatriated earnings. Naturally, it created no jobs; it was never intended or expected to. A second example comes from the 2003 discussion about Medicare drug coverage. If legislators proposed that drug companies compete for the government's business the way other industries do, this was called "price controls". The reason this sort of gross mischaracterization keeps happening is that it works. Taxpayers have to pay a lot to keep industry noncompetitive, which it then calls "free-market capitalism".

Another abuse of the language is the use of *"reform"*, when no such thing is meant. Reform is not expansion or subsidy or bailout; it is fundamental change. This is not occurring, either on Wall Street or in health care. What is happening instead is a lot of building up, cementing in place, and wealth transfer from the public to the people at the top, to the people who created the mess. This approach to "reform" is why the Obama administration may already be compromised. It is its war in Iraq, that thing which destroys credibility.

The lies discussed in this book keep getting told, over and over, and they keep working; we keep going along with them. There is little about the 2008 election that brought change. We saw this first from some early Cabinet appointments, then from the continued Wall Street bailout, then from the health care plan. The latter started by first assuring the insurance and drug industries that they would be unimpaired, if not benefited, and then moving on to less critical constituencies. For example, assuming no public option, at this writing, health insurers stand to get $500–$800 billion in federal subsidies. In return, they can no longer deny customers coverage, or adjust their premiums, for preexisting conditions, or set benefit caps. But otherwise there is no change in the system, which is a huge win for the same faction that helped produce the crisis.

This book may sound liberal or Democratic. But the point is bigger than that; it is not partisan or political. The point is, we now have the best government money can buy. Its only agenda is, and will continue to be, to serve and protect big money, with the public kept distracted by all manner of extraneous stuff—

preferably no more wars, but one sort of program after another. Big money must love all the partisanship and political division; it is all so wonderfully beside the point.

In a country not driven by the big-money agenda, criteria for personnel would not be that Congress has faith in them, or that they can hit the ground running, and we need someone right away because this is a crisis. The time to embrace principle is exactly when it is not expedient to do so. That is what principle is, and it is what is needed above everything else, especially in a crisis.

Second, no measures should be adopted or even considered that are at heart relief for, or benefits to, screwups, at the expense of everyone else. When the people voted for change, that was precisely the change they were expecting. They were voting for a return to accountability, and an end to lying and corruption.

Third, regulation must be restored to respectability. It is not an epithet. Treating regulation as a bad thing is how it got Fematized. This degrading process is how banks became investment banks; investment banks became hedge funds; hedge funds became banks. Regulation should not be the responsibility of the Fed, which has surrendered its authority to oversee anything.

Fourth, the Federal Reserve Board, which is the principal agent of instability, should be got rid of, not replaced with a different group—just abolished.

Fifth, we really should catch Osama, even if he is in the mountains. If we can disrespect France all over the place, we should be able to challenge Pakistan to help us here.

Sixth, if there are 52,000 tax evaders at UBS, we should not settle for nabbing 4,450 of them. Our Justice and Treasury Departments both need to keep going until they get them all, regardless of any bizarre Swiss distinctions. We should also take back all the tens of billions our government paid under the table to Goldman Sachs.

None of these things will actually happen. The arsonists will go on running the fire department. Nothing can happen until we get publicly financed campaigns, or at least real limits on campaign spending. That was always the risk, we now know, of allowing extreme inequality of income and wealth—not that it was objectionable aesthetically so much as that we would become a plutocracy, no more democratic than eighteenth-century France or czarist Russia.

In the meantime, we will go on being controlled by lies, including the ones described in this book. Being successful will depend on one's ability and willingness to state things that are simply not true. Practice saying the lies over and over, confidently, assertively. Get other people to say them along with you. If you are questioned, get angry, claim privileged information, call for unity, disparage your opponent, do whatever is necessary, but keep repeating the statement. Stay on message. Eventually, others will simply go along. Your prospects will improve accordingly.

After a little while, though, if we all keep doing it, this will become a risky course, if it produces a final breakdown of trust in our institutions. A broad-based cynicism may already be forming. Maybe not citizens throwing bricks down the street yet, or setting parked cars on fire, but something not far removed. Perhaps a taxpayer revolt, peaceful to start, organized by perfectly respectable citizens just saying they have had enough. Bizarrely, participants may even include some of the nine out of twenty Americans who pay no income taxes and who have little to complain about. They might say they can no longer support our national agenda of a) serving the people at the top, and b) telling the most fantastic lies about how necessary it all is.

More and more regular employees will go on company books as 1099 outside contractors, so employers can avoid paying Social Security, Medicare, and unemployment insurance taxes, while employees avoid withholding and can reduce taxable income by either underreporting or claiming deductions. Let something like that get started, and there are real problems.

The only way to avoid that outcome—and it had better start very soon—is for everyone to start telling the truth. Self-indulgent negligence and corruption, it turns out, are not, after all, a wellspring of good fiscal or monetary or regulatory or public health or executive compensation policy. They are not some bright idea; they are the problem.

They have, however, been put forward with a hugely successful propaganda campaign. Anyone not on board is easily shouted down. This group think makes chances of reform low. For years, America has been told that a strong economy depends on a lot of borrowing and consuming; that regulation is a threat to capitalism; that tax cuts spur business investment; that the health care issue is who pays for it; that executive compensation must be lavish to retain top talent; that stockholders are owners; that today's Wall Street is vital to the economy.

None of this stuff is any truer than the ones about Iraq. A whole generation now needs to be reeducated. Otherwise, we are only painting over the underlying rot, when it all needs to be bored out and fresh wood glued in its place. But the shouters will be out in force to stop it.

The plutocracy is almost across the board. This book looks at it mostly from the business and financial perspective, because that is what I know best, having worked in this sphere for thirty-five years, and because that sector is so visibly outrageous today. But it extends elsewhere—for example, the really big grab called defense. Bill Moyers has found it even in our judiciary system. The final chapter of this book, Lie 7, finds it in the food we eat. When it robs us of our health, maybe that is when we stand up to it.

Lie 1.

The Way to Grow the Economy Is to Stimulate the People at the Top.

Trickle-down economics is a lie that has dominated economic policy for more than thirty years now. It says that tax cuts targeted at the people on top will stimulate business investment and entrepreneurship and thereby create jobs and economic growth. All the empirical evidence to the contrary has not been sufficient to discourage the telling of this one. It is the all-purpose big-money lie—if you give me special treatment, others will benefit, so it is in their interests and on their behalf that I want my favored status. In fact, unless I get my specially carved-out graft, I might just lie down on the job, and then God knows what will happen to the American way itself.

The whole argument is transparently silly, or we should urgently be giving breaks to police, firefighters, doctors, and nurses.

Otherwise, they all might become dispirited, discouraged from risk-taking, and lie down on the job. It is a marvel today that everybody who does not get capital gains treatment on their earned income does not just go out on strike, shouting, "Enough! Enough of all your bull! We want to be *incentivized* too." The country now is like one of its big companies—a never-ending river of incentive schemes, performance awards, and retention bonuses for the people at the top, without which they would presumably feel disinclined to do their jobs, combined with a chronically underfunded pension plan for everyone else.

I particularly enjoy the references to entrepreneurship in this connection, since this is something I know a little about firsthand. People become entrepreneurs for a variety of reasons. They may have a need to do it their way, and that need cannot be met inside someone else's structure. Or they may just be bad as employees. Or they may have no alternative. (In my case, all three.) But one thing that does not enter into the deliberations, ever, is a consideration of tax implications. That is just laughable. Tax planning and entrepreneurship are not on the same page; tax considerations do not weigh on the decision to be an entrepreneur. Maybe they should enter in, but they do not.

Still, smart people are just as vocal as ever on trickle-down, as fatuous as it is, so it needs to be addressed. Take the cuts early in the decade on both dividends and capital gains. The tax cut on dividends was supposed to incentivize higher payouts, while the cap gains cut was to stimulate business investment. This was an obvious contradiction. Even if one grants the efficacy of tax incentives (for which there is little historical evidence), they were clearly not operable here, since the two impulses being stimulated are mutually exclusive and would logically cancel each other out. If business investment grows, then liquidation, which is what dividends are, must slow down, and vice versa; incentivizing both capital gains and dividends together is not logically possible. And in the event, following the tax cuts, business investment collapsed, and dividends have been partly replaced with share repurchases. Transparently, the cuts were only about reducing taxes on wealth.

A point about share repurchases. They are not an "investment" or an expression of management's confidence in the outlook, or any such thing. They are the opposite—a slow-motion liquidation of the firm, exactly like dividends. Cash goes down on the left-hand side of the balance sheet, equity goes down on the right, and the firm gets smaller. The stock price may or may not go up in response, but there has been no investment, only disinvestment. Capital appreciation is not the same thing as capital formation. All dividends and share repurchases mean is that the management has run out of capital formation ideas, or at least does not have the patience for them.

Similarly, capital gains cuts do not stimulate investment; they stimulate cashing out. They facilitate doing private equity deals, which have to start with a seller. As with dividends and share repurchases, private equity deals are enabled by reinvesting cash flow below depreciation, which means an accelerated liquidation of the firm, which means job loss and economic drag. After years of watching exactly this scenario unfold, it is incredible that the liars are still beating their trickle-down drum, even with business investment and job creation having collapsed to record lows.

These tax cuts are just a sop to the rich, in the same way as cutting inheritance taxes. The same is true for the 15 percent capital gains tax rate on hedge fund and private equity fee income. In the first half of 2007 alone, private equity and hedge funds spent $5.5 million lobbying for a 15 percent tax rate. As an entrepreneur myself, I know a little about risk-taking, putting up my own capital, and creating jobs, having done it for sixteen years. For just as long, I had to pay taxes at ordinary income rates on my K-1 earnings. The reason was that I never got big enough to buy a U.S. senator. Fee income masquerading as capital gain is polluting what little remains of America's sense of fair play.

The plutocrats also say that U.S. corporate tax rates are too high; at 35 percent, they say, these rates are higher than in other countries, which is driving investment offshore. That is plainly false. Because of all sorts of loopholes—calling profit "international" when it is not (drug companies); "research" tax credit on spending that is marketing expense mislabeled; current taxes turned into deferred and never paid—corporate taxes actually paid to the federal government are unbelievably low. For example, at Dow Chemical, total tax provisions for the three years 2006 through 2008 were $3.066 billion. During that period, Federal income taxes actually paid were $447 million. In other words, the 35 percent statutory rate may or may not be high, but the truth of the matter is that the United States is a corporate tax haven for big multinationals.

Between 2004 and 2008, Pfizer says it got 88 percent of its income from overseas. This, despite charging the highest nonnegotiated prices for its drugs (e.g., Lipitor) in the United States. How can this be? Pharmaceutical companies can transfer new drugs to a holding company in the Caymans, shifting huge amounts of income out of the United States and into offshore tax havens (*NYT*, February 4, 2010). Drugmakers, and multinationals generally, have one of those bizarre groups, this one called Promote America's Competitive Edge, to camp out in Washington to defend this stuff.

In November 2009, something called the "Worker, Homeownership, and Business Assistance Act" became law. It extended unemployment benefits and renewed the first-time homebuyer tax credit. What it also did—what it really did—was give a $33 billion tax break to big business. It let big companies offset 2008 and 2009 losses against profit from as far back as 2004. This provision, which was hidden from view within the bill, will do nothing to grow the economy or create jobs. It is just another giveaway to big money, which is why it could not stand on its own. Before our government can do something worthwhile, there first has to be a big payoff to people who need it least.

Lie 2.

Loose Money Is Another Way to Grow the Economy.

The pusher came to the neighborhood over twenty years ago. He got the community hooked by offering the drug very cheaply. He regulated the drug lords, and he had the full cooperation and support of the authorities, who had been bought by the drug lords. All was well for a time. Then the drug lords got greedy. They dispensed too much to their friends. They cut some bad stuff into the pure stuff, bad enough to kill. Also, the pusher's demand expanded faster than the supply being brought into the neighborhood. There was talk in the community of maybe having to take the cure. Some people tried kicking the habit.

After a while, everyone was really starting to feel the painful effects of withdrawal. So the drug lords and the authorities met to decide what to do. They turned to the pusher. The pusher went into his lab and made a lot of junk synthetically. In just one month he put out stuff with a street value of one trillion dollars. He rushed the new bags out onto the street. And, within several months, the addict seemed much improved. Everyone commented on it, how well the addict was responding, how his situation seemed to have bottomed. The media played their part by offering a lot of distractions. And the drug lords and the authorities kept control of the neighborhood.

****

The chairman of the Federal Reserve regularly appears before Congress, where he promises to use monetary policy to provide economic growth without inflation. Congress, for its part, speechifies in favor of Fed ease (loose money) and generally praises the chairman for furnishing it. These appearances propagate at least two popular myths. One is that the Fed answers to the people, that the general population is the master it serves. The other is that loose money promotes economic growth.

The truth is, monetary looseness has by now, after over two decades of it, all but killed the American economy. It has been in force and remains so today, because it is what Wall Street wants. The chief drug lord who oversees all this mayhem and pronounces it good is the Federal Reserve, whose chairmen have the public so fooled they keep getting reappointed to more terms by presidents of both parties. In the recent past, trillions of newly printed dollars have gone to Wall Street and the banks, which are the masters the Fed serves, and almost none into the general economy (see Lie 6, "Bailing out Wall Street Was Necessary to Preserve the System").

It was not always this way. Earlier Fed chairmen tried, pretty successfully, to moderate economic swings and prevent bubbles and busts, yielding a "golden age" after World War II of over forty years of well-regulated markets in a sound economy.

One source of much wisdom here is the original *Star Trek* series from the late 1960s. In one episode, Mr. Scott has climbed into one of the ship's crawl spaces to effect some sort of repair. He is talking by communicator to Mr. Spock, who is on the bridge, thinking. Mr. Spock tells Mr. Scott to reverse polarity, to which Scotty says, "Are ye daft, man, ye'll blow us all up!" Spock says, "Proceed, Mr. Scott, I will explain." Naturally, reversing the polarity saves the day.

Mr. Spock would look at our situation today and recognize that perpetually loose Fed policy does not work, so going on with it, especially harder and faster, is not logical. Lowering the federal funds rate (a short-term rate and the only one the Fed adjusts) lowers the cost of borrowing for banks, prime brokers, and hedge funds, who borrow to build assets and take leveraged positions, but not for the rest of us. Persistent, unrestrained easy money raises the profits for the money changers, who use the cheap funds to inflate asset bubbles and financial markets, but it does not lower the rates for others. It does not affect rates on car loans or credit cards or mortgages, so it has no effect on the real economy.

For a while, the economy got some stimulation indirectly from this asset-inflating effect, but this was only inadvertent. The Fed serves its masters, the banks, and they will only reduce long-term rates, the ones at which the real economy borrows, if they decide to reduce their own net interest margin—i.e., their profits. They do not often decide to reduce their own profits, so Fed policy and the economy are perpetually delinked, unrelated.

In September 2007, Jon Stewart interviewed Alan Greenspan and was able, as no one else has been, to bring out the corrupt nature of the Federal Reserve. Mr. Greenspan seemed to have completely missed it, which was not a first for him.

> Jon: And so we're really just deciding, because when you lower interest rate and drive money to the stocks, that lowers the return people get on the savings.

> Alan: Ah, yes, yes indeed.

> Jon: So they've made a choice. We would like to favor those who invest in the stock market and not those that invest in the bank, that helps us.

> Alan: No, that's the way it comes out, but that's not the way it really is.

> Jon: But explain that to me because it seems that we favor investment, but we don't favor work. The vast majority

of people work and they pay payroll taxes, and they use banks. And then there's this whole other world of hedge funds and short betting, and it seems like craps, and they keep saying don't worry about it, free market, that's why we live in those much bigger houses. But it really isn't, it's the Fed or some other thing. No?

Alan: You know, I think you'd better reread my book.

This exchange illustrates the way the plutocracy answers truth when it encounters it—with a combination of double-talk, misdirection, and conceit, never a hint of misgiving. The chairman went on with a spiel about a sound money system, reducing uncertainty, human nature, how people interact, and economic activity. It appeared to make no sense either to Jon Stewart or to his audience.

A persistently low Fed funds rate serves an economy based on asset inflation, but the main benefits accrue to finance, to those whose business is borrowing short and lending long. The low borrowing cost to prime brokers and hedge funds is an obvious boon. The cost of servicing bridge loans and leveraged loan commitments on private equity deals is also low, allowing the fund managers to maintain positions and go on collecting fees, and to make distributions to themselves with borrowed money.

All this is to the good, but mainly for the money changers, for the financing activity itself. Contrary to the rhetoric, economic growth is not related to, or dependent on, this activity. All that hedge funds or private equity funds or proprietary trading desks do is churn real assets, which never grow, but just get passed around. If anything, that turnover produces and feeds on layoffs, which are called cost-cutting synergies. This is the activity the Federal Reserve serves, the one it cares most about—the pointless commotion of the financial whirl itself—which it is afraid of slowing.

So, this is today's financial system, the one the Fed pats itself on the back for preserving. How did it come to be this way? A low Fed funds rate created the whole monster.

Pre-Greenspan, banks used to attract deposits. They had to, in order to fund their business. Banks then took the depositors' money and used it to make loans. The interest rate on deposits had to be enough to incentivize savings, which it generally was. Savers used to buy CDs, for example, that yielded 6 percent or more. There was a positive savings rate—people spending less than their income—as a result of these rates.

Saving is really important to a healthy economy. Sustainable full employment comes from healthy business investment, which comes from savings. In fact, business investment equals savings—they are two sides of the same coin; they move together. So, if we cancel terms, we get: full employment comes from healthy savings, and, conversely, zero or negative savings produces zero or negative business investment.

For years now, Fed policy has been aimed at encouraging consumption, which has squelched saving. By 2008, the savings rate actually turned negative, and so did business investment. That is, capital outlays were less than liquidations through dividends, stock repurchases, and mergers. This produced a steadily declining manufacturing base and jobs, which is the problem with the economy. The weak job market has been blamed on technology, Mexican immigrants, and imports from China. The real villain is the Greenspan-Bernanke Fed. Most remarkably, our Fed then accuses other countries of saving too much, and not getting with the borrow-and-spend program. The real problem is that the United States is in liquidation, a mathematical necessity resulting from two decades of the Fed squelching saving.

A major multinational company recently bragged about having cut its capital spending in half. The CEO was practically shouting as he boasted about this. This is prevalent today—negative capital formation and therefore negative job growth. In the long run, job cuts come from capital formation cuts. And the negative capital formation is the mathematical, necessary outcome of a Fed policy that stifles savings. In other words, persistent Fed ease destroys jobs. It is not an economic stimulant; it is a very potent suppressant.

It gets worse. The Fed's brutal, long-term assault on America comes from three other directions. One is the devastating impact on savers from getting a rate that is, after tax at least, below the inflation rate.

Here we have to pause to define terms, especially inflation. Someday, some smart person is going to win the Nobel Prize for redefining inflation to include the all-in cost of living. That is, not just the cost of getting through today, but the extended cost of living. The consumer price index ("CPI") does the former, but it does not measure inflationary expectations, the cost of living that is assumed in the future.

To measure this, it will be recognized first that the cost of future consumption is the cost of saving. Saving is just delayed consumption, so we may measure the extended, present and future, cost of living by adding the cost of saving to the CPI. At this writing, in 2009, a huge bubble is being reflated in financial assets across the board, driven by the unbelievably loose Fed. Stocks, bonds, commodities, currencies, you name it, are all soaring in price to levels unrelated to objective value, which is to say, their cost is rising steeply, and with them the cost of saving. To put it another way, the return on saving is collapsing, compliments of a loose Fed. So, the extended, present plus future, cost of living will be murderously high, regardless of what the CPI says today.

Second, securitization. In the absence of good, old-fashioned bank deposits, which were stifled by puny returns, bank lending had to be financed somehow. The solution was selling loans to investment banks, which packaged them up and sold them again to investors, in a process now quite familiar. This whole machine was the spawn of a bank deposit shortage. Securitized debt came to account for 60 percent of all credit in the United

States. Securitization supplied the cash to loan originators. But underneath all the razzle-dazzle, no capital formation takes place, just capital appreciation. A lot of it.

Progressive rate cuts meant progressive downward pressure on deposits, which meant more and more securitization just to keep lending flat. And placing more and more of it meant everybody winking at quality. As it had to, the Ponzi scheme broke. Nobody will buy the stuff anymore, so the Fed had to step in. It is now printing trillions of dollars to buy securities that no one else will (see Lie 6). The whole rickety structure requires that assets be priced higher than private buyers will pay, with the government making up the difference. This is called free-market capitalism, even though the Fed is now financing all U.S. housing by being the only buyer of new mortgages.

All this commotion is not producing much activity in the real economy. Whether or not it was ever intended to may be debated. If it was intended to, then we must conclude that the Fed is incompetent; more likely, it was not intended to. In any case, house prices have only bumped along a bottom, about one-third below the 2006–2007 peaks. Lenders are not increasing their lending, nor corporations and consumers their borrowing, in a liquidity trap that was perfectly predictable. Instead, the oceans of newly printed money have spilled into the financial industrial complex, making whole the players who made the mess.

So, securitization has replaced deposits, the Fed's printing press is working furiously to keep the system from reverting to something healthy, and capital appreciation has replaced capital formation. A corollary is that for all this to happen there had to be a lot of deregulation (see Lie 5, "Regulation is Bad; Deregulation is Good"), including repealing Glass-Steagall (the law separating nonlending activities from deposit-taking), so that banks could become investment banks; investment banks, hedge funds; and hedge funds, banks.

Third, financialization, redistribution, and attendant wealth disparity. The Fed has repeatedly gone into crisis mode, not to fight inflation, but to fight deflation. By doing so, it has kept real wages artificially low while boosting profit and inflating asset values, whereas a kind of benign, supply-driven deflation, which was otherwise occurring, would have meant rising real incomes. The result has been a huge shift in the relative returns on work (down) and capital (up). A massive real wealth transfer upward has taken place (not because of NAFTA or China or technology or immigration) from wages and salaries and benefits to asset ownership, from earned income to unearned. Distortions wrought by financialization have also diverted a whole generation of our best and brightest into becoming money changers instead of doing something useful.

In 2009, our government has blessed and sanctified this choice. The message is, if you are in the business of making things, you should get reeducated, retrained. If you are in finance, we will make it our highest national priority to keep you whole. This is not really surprising—once the financial economy has been created, it must be served and protected, like Frankenstein's monster. The financial industrial complex has understandably developed a remarkable sense of entitlement; at no time has it ever said the Fed funds rate might be too low.

A couple of years ago, Alan Greenspan said he worried about populism forcing too much Fed looseness. That was insincere, even for him. The perpetual Fed ease he brought has devastated America.

So, what should monetary policy be? When a bad policy produces catastrophe, Mr. Spock would say that doing more of the same, only harder and faster, will not redeem it. All we are doing now is making an historically big mistake bigger. (The worst of it is, everyone knows this, but it goes on anyway, because of what James Grant, editor of *Interest Rate Observer*, calls socialism for the rich. The modern Fed knows what master it serves.)

Monetarism said policy should be to maintain stable money supply growth. So said Milton Friedman, but then targeting money supply growth was discredited. (Friedman was a very clever man, but it is hard to recall his being right about something.) Then came inflation targeting—setting a desired rate and aiming for it. That is not right, either, we now know. In a world in which all the forces would otherwise have yielded a kind of benign deflation, or mildly dropping prices, this kind of targeting was just deflation-fighting, asset-inflating, and real wage-reducing. The mess we are in now comes from chronically loose money and cheap and easy credit, which in turn comes from inflation-targeting at a time when there was no more threat from inflation than from Mars, or Iraq.

Years from now, our Nobel Prize winner will present a new policy thesis. That is, the goal should be to balance the impulse to borrow and the impulse to save. Not perpetually goose the former and stifle the latter, with foreign lenders and securitization making up the difference, but hold them in tension. A CD earning 2 percent, or a savings account earning half a percent, is just a disincentive to save, which starves capital investment, job creation, and economic growth. Business investment drops below depreciation; liquidation replaces capital formation, etc., all because the impulse to save has been squelched. Leverage builds up and up; consumption depends on asset prices; so the country has the tiger by the tail.

As for what to do now, Mr. Spock would say, reverse the polarity. Increase the Fed funds rate by 50 basis points per quarter for the next three years, until it reaches 6 percent. Announce now that this is the plan, and that it is unconditional, with no Fed meetings or deliberation or flexibility around it.

Such a move would take the Fed out of the equation—an enormous positive in itself—and would eliminate uncertainty. The principal downside would be the massive job loss resulting from laying off the whole Fed-watching industry. But bank deposits would be rebuilt, and with them, sound lending, capital formation, and job creation. All we are doing now is producing the opposite, in an expensive and futile effort to extend a hugely overextended credit supercycle and transferring more wealth upward by reflating financial assets.

The Fed's charge includes seeing to the well-being of the banks. The modern Fed needs to drop its present interpretation of that charge, and adopt a new one. The new one would include helping the banks attract deposits so that banking itself makes sense again. That is, stimulate savings. But, not to worry, it will never happen.

Lie 3.

The Stock Market Is the Best Investment, and an Indicator of the Economy.

In December, 2009, Alan Greenspan told Bloomberg News that the stock market rally had lessened the need for more economic stimulus. He said capital gains were providing greater stimulus than the stimulus program. Back on planet Earth, however, the only real stimulus has come from the $300 billion peanut spent so far under that program, on aid to states and infrastructure.

One of the most pervasive myths around is the one that asserts that the stock market and the real economy are connected in any meaningful way. Actually, the stock market is just the stock market. It is its own reality. It does drive a lot of other things, like Fed policy, which gives it an aura of primacy, but it is disconnected from the lives of all but a few.

The real economy can sink below the horizon, which will call forth earnest-sounding speeches from policy makers. But let the stock market sink, and that produces emergency response. Senior officials will hold hastily-convened meetings, even over the weekend, and commit enormous public resources to address the problem, and announce this new commitment before the market opens in Asia on Monday morning.

How did we get to this point, at which we have been brainwashed to believe in a linkage that is not there? The answer can be traced to two sublies.

One is that there is a big, broad "investor class" that includes most of the population. The most recent claim has it at 56 percent, but it has been put higher. Anyway, a big percentage of people are said to own stocks "directly or indirectly". The lie here is manifest even before adding the "or indirectly" part. The good citizen who has a $50,000 401-K and a $250,000 mortgage is not really in the same boat as the guys with mail sacks full of stock-based "incentives". The total value of all defined contribution plan assets, $1.93 trillion at this writing, is a rounding error in the $53.4 trillion household net worth. There is a 401-K class, and there is a stock-option class, and the two are not living on the same planet, let alone sharing membership in the same class.

Meanwhile, the "or indirectly" group must refer to pension plan participants. Use of this phrase neglects to mention that pension beneficiaries do not share in any stock market upside. Participants in defined benefit plans are just that—their benefit is defined. The stock market can double or quintuple, but they will experience no change in their situation. The pension plan sponsor will, but not the plan beneficiary. In any case, ownership, real participation in the stock market, is concentrated in the hands of a few, and fewer all the time.

The second sublie is that the stock market is there to raise capital for a growing economy. Of course, that does happen. This is the stock market at its best, as the key ingredient in capitalism. The higher share prices are, the cheaper it is for firms to raise equity financing, so they invest more in their businesses, which grows the economy and creates jobs. Examples of this occurring are many and obvious, and they demonstrate how desirable it is to have a healthy, fully valued stock market.

However, in today's economy, businesses are net liquidators (see Lie 2, "Loose Money Is Another Way to Grow the Economy"). They distribute more, on balance, through dividends, share repurchases, mergers, and private equity deals, all of which are capital-extractive, than they invest. Share repurchases may drive up share prices, but they are not "investments"; cash goes down on the left-hand side of the balance sheet, and equity goes down on the right, and the result is an entity less able to invest. The stock market god demands this; it is called "optimizing shareholder value".

The liquidation process inflates the value of management's stock options, and it produces dividends to private equity, but it chokes off investment, growth, and jobs. Today's stock market is not an engine of the economy; it is its braking system. The stock market is no longer primarily a source of capital for growth; it is an exit strategy, a liquidation mechanism. Since 1991, according to Grant Thornton, the number of U.S. exchange-listed companies is down by 22 percent. Adjusted for real GDP growth, the decline is a staggering 53 percent. This means that the number of buyouts and mergers has exceeded intitial public offerings by a lot, which puts the lie to the stock market as capital-raising device myth. It is the reverse, and associated U.S. job losses are estimated at 22 million.

Interestingly, even with all the commotion and machinations around it, this modern stock market has not been particularly rewarding to average investors. Let's say such an investor started in 1995 to put in $5,000 every year, so he/she is dollar cost-averaging, and has done this faithfully for fifteen years. Let's also assume that the money went into an S&P 500 index fund, a low-cost, well-diversified vehicle for stock market investing, and the purchases were made on June 30 every year, so that each "share" had a cost equal to the index level on that day. So, no silly attempts at market-timing. Finally, let's assume (wrongly, no doubt, but for simplicity) that there are no reinvested dividends, or dividend taxes, fees, commissions, or expenses.

In other words, the investor did everything right and did it faithfully for fifteen years, starting in June 1995 and ending in June 2009. The investor has a cost in his or her portfolio today of $75,000. With that money, he/she has acquired 73.22 "shares". At this writing, the index is at 1210, so the portfolio is now worth $88,600. So, the return is 18 percent for the whole period, or just 2 percent a year.

This is quite remarkable. The investor would have done far better just rolling over CDs and paying taxes on the interest along the way.

In the current era, the stock market works wonderfully, but mainly for two groups. One, of course, is the people in the business of selling the stock market to everybody else. They make unimaginable sums every year. Investors would do better if so much were not siphoned off by the money changers in fees of all sorts, including insider trading profits (see Lie 5, "Regulation Is Bad; Deregulation Is Good"). When people say Wall Street is essential to the economy, they mean it is essential to itself, which has become a big part of the economy.

The other group the stock market serves is the stock-option class, that is, top management. This group does not have to invest up front and hope for the best, the way everyone else does. It can wait until the Fed boosts the stock above the exercise price and then sell for an immediate, risk-free profit. This is called aligning management's interest with shareholders'.

If the investor has been using a 401-K, he/she is really in the hole. When that money is withdrawn at retirement, it will all be taxed on the way out at ordinary income rates, so the $88,600 portfolio is worth no more than $70,000. Tax rates may be lower in retirement than before, or they may not; they may be higher.

So, assuming our investor did everything right, the whole exercise was pointless, and the big winner was Wall Street.

If there is one lesson from the past couple of years, or decades, it is that the stock market is a fraud. It is an inside game played by and for the people who already have all the chips. The investing public is the sap at the table. The government is on the house's side. This subject is of paramount importance today. The new president himself has not grasped it; witness his indefensible appointments to head Treasury and the SEC. Both of the people appointed were a big part of the problem, of the corrupt mess we are in.

The biggest evidence of this is the rules themselves. The rules say that fund managers and Wall Street executives and corporate managements win big on the way up, but investors and taxpayers take the hit on the way down. Any eight-year-old has the sense not to play in such a rigged game. If a hedge fund returns 15 percent a year for three years and drops 35 percent in year four, the investor makes zero before fees and is down 16 percent after fees, and the manager is a huge winner and closes down the game. If a "financial institution" earns reported profits for three years, and then in year four there are losses that offset all those cumulative prior earnings, the executives and traders gorge on bonuses, maybe foregoing one, under pressure, in year four, and the investors and taxpayers get left holding the bag.

So there is an unimaginable amount of graft and corruption in the whole stock market swindle. By now, this is well understood by all. And granted, our government is on the side of protecting the house against both investors and taxpayers. Still, even with all that, is it not surprising that investors do not do better?

There are a couple of possible explanations. One we have discussed in Lie 2—namely, the prevailing business model in recent times, which has been to liquidate in slow motion. This model, which hedge funds and other institutions insist that managements adopt, involves turning the assets of the company into cash, by either selling or borrowing against them, and paying it out. It turns out that this so-called value optimization process is not, after all, productive of sustainable long-term gains. Disinvesting is better than a company investing badly, but this latter should not be management's bogey, as it has become.

Then, there is stock ownership itself. The lore here is that top management reports to, is answerable to, the Board of Directors. The Board is elected by the shareholders, so the management reports to shareholders. If there is something shareholders want, they can propose it, vote on it at the annual meeting, and, if it passes, management will abide by it. Shareholders can also be reassured by "incentive" plans, which align the interests of management with their own.

None of this is true. The Board is appointed by, paid by, and serves at the pleasure of, management. It is there to protect the interests of management from the shareholders. It guarantees to management compensation packages that accrue regardless of outcome for shareholders. In the unlikely event of a stockholder proposal being passed, management and the Board are free to reject it.

In fact, management reports to itself and does so untroubled by any concern for shareholders. It is important to acknowledge what this means, namely, that shares of stock are claims on nothing; they represent ownership of nothing. They are themselves derivatives, like credit default swaps. They have no more reality than the green and red symbols flickering on LED screens. If you doubt this, companies and their immunized Boards have legions of lawyers ready to explain it to you.

When this whole farce collapses, it may be from e-mails, which are the instrument of undoing for a lot today. Even very smart people put things in e-mails they should not. Recently, it came out that one Bank of America director e-mailed another in connection with the Merrill Lynch deal. Management wanted the deal, so the Board got behind it. The e-mail read, "Unfortunately, it's screw the shareholders!!"

This is the true nature of the relationship between managements and their boards and the shareholders. Managements are the owners, and Wall Street serves them faithfully. Mergers and acquisitions advisors are always, always in favor of deals, even though they all go bad for the company and the country, and then a new management has to come in to repair the damage. But the Board stays on, and the old management leaves, incredibly rich.

It is amazing that the stock market sells as high as it does. It would not, except for all the heroic exertions on its behalf by the Fed, plus a whole lot of layoffs.

****

So, how should we invest? Own mutual funds, a lot of them. Own stock mutual funds, bond funds, balanced funds. Own big-cap and small-cap, foreign and domestic, long-term and short-term, taxable and tax-free. This way, whatever your Sharpe ratio (the return on a portfolio divided by the swings in its value) is, the denominator will be very, very low. In other words, diversify, far more than anyone says to. The percent that is in stocks should be one hundred minus your age. If you are fifty-seven, for example, and own fourteen mutual funds in equal size, six should be equity funds.

Buy no-load mutual funds from Wellington/Vanguard, T. Rowe Price, Black Rock, American Funds, Oppenheimer. No hedge funds or ETFs (exchange traded funds)—you are not that dumb. No individual securities, which is obviously for suckers only. Average in over time—no market timing. Never sell. (The Fed will be along shortly to reflate; that is all it does.) To goose the numerator, use whatever cheap financing you can to add leverage, which you can do responsibly if you have truly diversified. You can never compete at this with the banks, who get no-cost money from the Fed that they are supposed to lend out but don't, but you can't worry about this.

Lie 4.

Executive Compensation Is Tied to Performance and Provides Incentive to Perform.

A constellation of lies surrounds the subject of management compensation:

- Executives need far greater incentives than other people do, or they might not perform.
- Executives also need to be retained, while others are laid off, because their talent is in short supply.
- Executives' compensation is variable and performance-based; the better job they do, the more they are paid.

Certainly by now it is clear that this is all poppycock. What is discouraging is that even with this widespread understanding, it goes on undisturbed and unchallenged! It is a bus barreling down the street, with everyone else just running alongside barking at the tires.

The most overworked, overstated concept today, at least as applied to compensation, may be "incentive". It is invoked constantly and everywhere. My experience as an employer, however, has been that people at work generally have a pretty fixed idea of the job they are willing to do and beyond which they are not willing to go. They also have a very definite idea about how much they need to make for doing that job. It is uncommon to interview anyone whose main concern is not whether they will be guaranteed that specific amount, independent of any measurement of performance. People seem to have a built-in level they are bound to perform at, and an equally rigid view of what they need to get paid, which all seems counter to the notion of incentives.

One "producer" I hired joined only on the basis of a $225,000 salary, guaranteed for three years. I interviewed another candidate in about 2000, when money was flowing on Wall Street like particles in a cyclotron. He was in his twenties and new to the industry. I asked him what he required, and he said he needed to be "visible on" $500,000 a year. I thanked him for coming in. After a number of similar episodes, I came to the view, which headhunters can attest, that not many people in the workplace actually want to be "incentivized". They want to know what they can be assured of getting.

My suspicion was confirmed in *Good to Great*, by Jim Collins, who says, "It's who you pay, not how you pay them." The author took compensation data from proxy statements and performed 112 separate analyses, looking for patterns and correlations—cash versus stock, long-term versus short-term incentives, salary versus bonus, etc. Comparing comparable companies on performance, he found "no systematic differences on the use of stock (or not), high salaries (or not), bonus incentives (or not), or long-term compensation (or not) ... " "We found no systematic pattern linking executive compensation to the process of going from good to great."

What the author argues, and which I can confirm, is that some people will perform above average just by the nature of who they are—not because they have been incentivized to do so but because their own moral code requires it. So, companies should try to get these people in the first place, rather than fiddle with pay packages. Such people need to be paid fairly and well and competitively, or they will feel taken advantage of, but the trick is to find the right people, not induce the right behavior.

So, when you hear compensation packages described in terms of its incentives, you may be sure you are listening to either a fool or a liar. After all, if incentives are such a good idea, why not apply them to teachers, police, firefighters, doctors, nurses, etc.?

Boards of directors have many times shown that they also reject incentives, in a story that has now been around more times than a fan belt. Nobody believes it, most especially not the people who reference it the most. Top management's packages are not just impossibly lush; they are all guaranteed. They are both huge and, more important, predetermined, set in airtight contracts before there has been any performance, good or bad. When the company falls apart, and after thousands of employees are laid off, the Board must still make good on every last cent of its contract. In extremis, if the Board is sufficiently embarrassed, publicly, management might have to be replaced, in which event it collects on another predetermined, contractually guaranteed package.

All the talk about performance-based incentives is just that—talk; it refers to nothing. Generally, the concept of incentive is overinvoked or misused. Private-equity deals and mergers are driven by guaranteed packages, which are then called incentive payments. A variant is the retention bonus, given to people who have no thought of leaving and no place to go. The rhetoric of incentives applied to entrepreneurship is certainly wrong—being an entrepreneur is something you are driven to do, not incentivized to do.

Guaranteed, noncontingent outcomes, we now know, are the accepted norm, which belies the whole notion of incentive. Lately, the incidents have related to Wall Street. Ken Lewis of Bank of America might get no severance, but he does have a $53 million pension and $82 million in stock, for a $135 million consolation prize. But the phenomenon of unconditional, guaranteed, out-of-control packages is not exclusively or even mainly a Wall Street issue.

In May 2007, Northwest Airlines came out of bankruptcy, after twenty months of jamming employees for $2.4 billion a year. Douglas M. Steenland, the CEO, got a $25 million package. The employees were furious, almost defeating the plan. An interview with Steenland at the time went:

Q. *Given how angry workers across the airline industry are about chief executive pay packages, why did you take such a big one?*

A. *The compensation process is not one I play a role in. The decisions were made by the Northwest Board of Directors, acting completely independently of management.*

Q. *But you could have insisted on less, just as you took reduced pay during the bankruptcy, right?*

A. *If you look at things on a relative basis, in 2006 compared to the other network CEOs, I was fifth out of six. Among Fortune 500 CEOs, I'm in the lower 50 percent.*

The exchange highlights fixtures of executive compensation. One is the sense of entitlement the CEO class feels, which others find bizarre, but which they see as only reasonable. Another is the lack of any reference to performance or results. For the CEO class, the only important measure is what they get compared to their peers. For them, a package is never big if there are others like it. Finally, there is the big lie: my Board of Directors did it, and I was powerless to stop them. Of course, I appointed them, and they and the compensation consultants get paid by me, but shucks, what am I to do?

The nadir in corporate governance was reached earlier this decade at Pfizer. There, the CEO, Hank McKinnell, destroyed not just "shareholder value", but other values as well. Products were overmarketed. Bad acquisitions were made in serial fashion. Litigation, advertising, lobbying, and cost-cutting (layoffs) substituted for innovation.

Pfizer's bad management even cost U.S. taxpayers, at least twice. The highest-return investments the company made, by far, were its political contributions. This resulted in, first, the Medicare drug bill, which I called the Pfizer Payback and Relief Act of 2003, a really ugly piece of legislation that hugely benefited drug companies, chiefly Pfizer. The White House defended this law with everything it had against all comers.

Second, and even better, was the American Jobs Creation Act. This law allowed repatriation of foreign earnings, untaxed, and represented a huge tax amnesty masquerading as an economic stimulus. Naturally, not a single job was created. The biggest beneficiary was Pfizer, whose tax forgiveness was $28 billion, and who then went on demonstrating that it had no earthly idea what to do with the money.

Pfizer in this decade has been an unmixed blight, not just on corporate America, but on the national landscape, not even counting the legalized tax evasion that happens every year from drug companies calling domestic earnings foreign.

Finally, in mid-2006, even the Board had had enough. Under extreme circumstances, and with great reluctance, it finally terminated the CEO. For laying waste not just to Pfizer but a good chunk of America, the CEO got his contractually obligated package of $249 million. This is the true nature of executive compensation in the twenty-first century. No double-talk here about incentive or pay for performance or aligning interests or defined contribution or ownership society; just straight, in-your-face entitlement.

It is worse than that. The system seems to select for a certain individual who is not quite human. Other people in the same situation, having produced so much mayhem, might say, "Hey, I'll just take $200 million, you keep the other $49 million." Or, if they were fully human, they might just leave. But not these people, oh no; give them every last cent, plus a car and driver. These are the people in charge.

How did they get this way? They probably did not start out as bad people, so something corrupted them. Part of it is stock options, by far the most dangerous and deceitful device in the business world. America will go on being a sinkhole of corruption until stock options are gotten rid of—not reformed, not disclosed, but gotten rid of.

The basic lie about stock options is that they align management interests with that of shareholders. This is obviously not true, or the investing public would be given a flock of options, to put them on the same footing as management. Stock options are a gift, pure and simple, from the shareholders to management, and a very costly one, at that.

By offering managements the chance at risk-free upside, stock options encourage them to shoot the moon, meaning a lot of deal-making. With each transaction come the claims about synergies and growth. In no case does any of it come true—not any aspect of it except the layoffs; on the contrary, it all goes terribly wrong, and shareholders suffer the fearful consequences for years.

Incidences of these things are so numerous that citing examples would simply be tedious. One, though, is too hard to resist. In 2009, Dow Chemical had a really ugly year—29 percent sales drop, several thousand layoffs—but the stock market rallied. The value of the CEO's option package octupled. Someone said that Vivaldi did not compose 611 concertos but that he wrote one concerto 611 times.

The same can be said of "strategic" mergers. The prime mover cannot be management incompetence—no managers can be that bad over and over again. It is stock options. They are not just an incentive; they are practically an inducement to roll the dice, since there is no risk to the holder of an adverse outcome. Worst case, it all goes smash, and the exec gets his or her enormous, predetermined, contractually guaranteed package. Conversely, there is enormous upside. After announcing the deal, management makes its presentation, does a road show, backed up and cheered by Wall Street. During this honeymoon, and long before it ends, the option holder can exercise and sell the shares.

A partial remedy would be to restrict option-related shares from sale for two or three years after exercise, so that managements had to wait, along with shareholders, to see how it all turned out. Also, require that options be uncancelable and exercised only in the order they were given, to prevent cozy repricings. The number of deals would plummet. Then the options rhetoric would make more sense. Until then, managements are the de facto owners. Public shareholders are owners in the same sense that baseball fans are the team owners. The powerful genius of private equity was just this: if you want to experience ownership, you have to get the business away from the managements and their boards.

Another stock options lie says that calculating the cost of options is difficult. Actually, it is quite simple. It takes no discounted present value assumptions or Black-Scholes higher math, just some fourth-grade arithmetic. Go to the sources and uses of funds statement. If the company used $200 million on share repurchases and raised $100 million from options exercised, then it used $100 million reducing its number of shares outstanding.

Now go to the balance sheet. If, over the period, the number of shares dropped by 2 million, then it was buying in stock at $50 a share. If the average price in the market over the period was twenty-five, repurchasing 2 million shares should have cost $50 million. So, there is a missing $50 million, which is the after-tax cost to shareholders in that period of the options program. It is the amount of cash flow generated by the business that is withheld from shareholders and diverted to management.

The amounts are always enormous and never reported. Of all the legions of analysts on Wall Street, no one calculates this effect. In economic terms, the savings from letting thousands of people go are transferred to management, to the applause of investors.

Shareholders either do not recognize the truly breathtaking nature of this expense, or have decided not to care. It is obscured by the use of generally accepted accounting (the best of today's flimflams are perfectly legal), a method no one can explain, defend, or understand. But the menace of stock options goes beyond the business world. The prodigious wealth created by stock options is also how America lost control of its government, why so many domestic programs put forward are either corporate welfare measures or tax cuts for the rich. (John Cassidy, in the *New Yorker* ("Goodbye to All That", September 15, 2003) says, "The federal government has been transformed into a political-action committee for the well-to-do.") A portion of these benefits gets rebated in the form of campaign contributions. Another portion goes to lobbyists and think tanks, which are now the same thing. The magic ingredient is an unlimited flow of money.

Another negative consequence of stock options is the Six-Sigma method of operational efficiency. They grew up together. Stock options reward rapid share price gains, and letting people go is the fastest way to produce share price gains. Six-Sigma is just another name for letting people go.

Jack Welch at GE got famous for being a great manager—he has written books about it. Jack started out his reign as Neutron Jack. He was called this because the people got nuked, but the buildings were left standing. The writings and teachings of Jack mainly amount to letting people go—one in ten every year. GE is famous for Six-Sigma. It may not be much of a stretch, then, to equate Six-Sigma and letting people go; that is what Six-Sigma is. (Jack no doubt grew tired of being called Neutron Jack.) It is a dressed-up thing that amounts to layoffs. In *Lethal Weapon*, the bad guy is talking about a shipment of merchandise, and Mel Gibson says, "Why don't you guys just call it heroin?" Six-Sigma has black belts and training and projects, but it amounts to headcount reduction.

Presentations to highlight Six-Sigma delineate the number of black belts and projects and how much the whole company is behind it, not about what it actually is. There is a close fit between Six-Sigma operating profit and headcount reductions multiplied by an estimate of per-employee costs. It may be belaboring the point, but Six-Sigma profits and layoffs are the same.

The problem with all this is that the savings are transferred to management, so it is a short-term wash unless investors fall for it, and they have stopped falling for it, which is why we have stopped hearing about Six-Sigma. No doubt, big business was overstaffed and productivity low, which was hurting returns, competitive position, etc. But the real challenge is a long-term one, namely, how to grow the business.

Stock options do not generally reward long-term growth. Instead, they work best for the holder who goes for a quick kill—who announces a "restructuring" or a "strategic" merger and sends out the minions to talk it up without having to wait around to see how it turns out. Only a fool would exercise an option and not immediately sell the shares, so the method induces only short-term measures.

It also reinforces the trend toward business liquidation. Corporations are not reinvesting even to cover depreciation and amortization and deferred taxes, so that free cash flow is even greater than profit. This accounts for all the share buybacks and all the private equity activity. In recent years, big business spent far more on stock repurchasing plus dividends than it did on capital investments. Corporations today are in fact liquidating because that is where all the rewards are for the stock-option class.

Management for the short run, induced by stock options, is unhealthy. After Six-Sigma was played out at GE, Jack Welch left. His successor, Jeff Immelt, then got the job of actually trying to grow the business. The stock has fallen completely apart. The only winner from all the commotion was Jack Welch, who made hundreds of millions, maybe a billion, dollars on his options. We would not even know this, except that it came out during his divorce.

A protégé of Jack's at GE was James McNerney, who brought Six-Sigma to 3M, where 8,000 people were let go in a few years. When the terminations were done, so was Six-Sigma, with costs minimized and margins at peak. Investors started to ask about growth, which is a lot harder than letting people go. Mr. McNerney, like his mentor, understood this. He moved on, impossibly rich on his 3M options, to be CEO at Boeing. His successor at 3M, George Buckley, has been trying to revive it since.

The U.S. economy today is just a very big GE or 3M—in layoff and liquidation mode. Management compensation, and stock options in particular, are part of the reason.

Lie 5.

Regulation Is Bad;
Deregulation Is Good.

Along with trickle-down and a loose Fed, the third leg of the stool in the big-money agenda is deregulation. It would be, for obvious reasons. But it has to be dressed up, like the other two. Regulation is self-evidently a good thing, like air traffic control or double yellow lines down the middle of the road. It is just essential for public safety, so it must be attacked in favor of deregulation. The shouters even make it an issue of patriotism, with deregulation not just an integral part of capitalism (it is what is meant by "free-market"), but even an article of being fully American. The basic pitch is that regulation makes America uncompetitive, while free markets (used as the euphemism for deregulation) make us competitive.

In March 2007, something really strange happened, quite surreal, like a donkey on top of a school bus. Treasury Secretary Paulson and SEC Commissioner Cox assembled a panel of big-money players to complain about overregulation of business and finance. It was part of a series of big-shot discussions, mostly behind closed doors, convened by the Bush administration. The evident agenda was to elicit sympathy for big business and Wall Street as they struggled under the yoke of excessive regulation, and to lobby for the rollback of laws they found irksome.

Dick Cheney kicked things off, naturally enough, by speaking to the "conference" at a private dinner sponsored by the Treasury department. A vivid imagination is not required to suppose that the message to big money was, have courage; we feel your pain; the officials in charge of the IRS, the SEC, the EPA, etc., are all people who feel you are being mistreated; we are committed to relieving you of your burden and overhauling the regulatory system.

Of course, the moment for coming to the rescue of big money had passed, probably for a very long time, but these people just have no such sensibility, or at least not compared to their insatiable, insistent greed. The agenda is remarkable on several levels.

First is the constant expression of concern about competitiveness, as in, business must be able to compete. This plea would be more persuasive if corporate profits were not at historic highs relative to GDP and business investment at new lows. In other words, unreinvested cash flows are at levels never before dreamed of. The idea that American business is uncompetitive is not compatible with its incredibly fat profit margins, or with its evident strategy of slow-motion liquidation.

Second, Wall Street in particular seems an odd object of sympathy. Financials' share of corporate profits is grotesquely out of line with either common sense or history. Maybe there is precedent for this, but not in the past eighty years. This is the consequence of the *financialization* of America—the replacement of both production and service with finance. The best and the brightest in our society now do private equity, or if they are second-best and brightest, hedge funds. The third-brightest "trade" fixed income at Wall Street firms, which means they let the Fed inflate the value of their inventory.

So, under Mr. Bush, businesses were able to bear up quite well, even under the burden of what Mr. Paulson called excessive regulation. SEC Commissioner Cox, who also saw relief for big business as a priority, stepped in on behalf of CEOs and reversed a ruling on disclosure of their compensation packages.

What is even more grotesque is that nothing has changed under Mr. Obama. It is very much business as usual, in every way. The Managed Funds Association ("MFA"), the hedge fund lobby, is as successful as ever in preventing regulation. It has meetings with Mr. Geithner, Mr. Bernanke, and Ms. Schapiro (SEC chair) to say that hedge funds pose no systemic risk to the economy.

This argument is accepted, despite the hedge funds becoming big, de facto lenders by buying securities. Aside from the federal government, hedge funds are today's banks, just as banks became investment banks, and investment banks became hedge funds. To call the structure out of control would be generous, and the taxpayer is backstopping it all. A former Treasury official who left first to lobby for the D. E. Shaw hedge fund group was elected to head the MFA and was joined by a former Republican congressman. Our government today serves the same masters no matter who is in the White House. Regulators, paid by the taxpayers, are not exactly The Untouchables, unless Elliot Ness took his orders from the gang leaders.

I found out firsthand about twenty-first-century regulation. My firm had a broker-dealer registered with NASD (National Association of Securities Dealers), later FINRA (Financial Industry Regulatory Authority). We were closely regulated and found the regulations arbitrary and needlessly punitive, as I told the head of NASD in a letter. But our biggest objection was that other firms in our business operated freely by simply not bothering to become members, thereby avoiding regulation altogether. This abuse was even expanded by an SEC ruling, at the behest of the big firms, allowing nonmembers to participate in "commission-sharing arrangements" (a previously disallowed practice) with big member firms. In a nutshell, the regulators did everything possible to drive small member firms out of business. Some regulation seems to exist because big players see it as a wonderfully clean way to impair small players more.

So, I take a backseat to no one in my contempt for the way regulation is sometimes handled today. But that does not point to deregulation. It is just a clever syllogism to say that, because regulation is practiced badly, the effort should be abandoned. Some very shrewd people have actually put forward the argument that regulation promises a clean, fair world, but it cannot deliver, so it should be dropped, which will prevent more disappointment.

The case is made even stronger if the people put in charge of regulatory bodies are either screwups or do not themselves believe in regulation. If they can botch the job sufficiently, that will hasten deregulation's day—in short, the FEMA strategy, and a very clever one it is: if we can do the job badly enough, the whole effort will be discredited, and then killed. Hence, at the SEC, replace William Donaldson, a believer in regulation, with Christopher Cox, a nonbeliever. It is the radical cousin of the one about killing government spending by creating really big deficits.

A case in point of such aggressive negligence is insider trading, which shows the extremes of deregulation today. Insider trading is both obvious and rampant, and well known. It is simply ignored, even when it is called to the regulators' attention.

In 2006, Delta and Pine Land stock rose 23 percent, in a straight line, between June 30 and August 14, compared with 0 percent at the time for stocks overall. On August 15, it was announced that the company would be acquired by Monsanto. This sort of thing was, as I recall it, common during the bubble years. Occasionally, some small fry got busted, as if to say there are a few bad apples in an otherwise good barrel. Aggressive deregulation, in the holy name of free markets, really meant the barrel was rotten. The stock market truly became an insiders' game.

But the point today is that nothing much has changed. High-profile or small-time, a few cases are reported, but the underlying beat goes on. In 2009, Dainippon Sumitomo Pharma of Japan said on September 3 that it was acquiring Sepracor for $2.6 billion in cash, or $23 per share. The day before, trading in the stock was halted after it jumped from $18 to $22.80 intraday.

These incidents pale by comparison with the trading history in Rohm and Haas stock. In July 2008, it saw really egregious insider trading previous to the announcement of Dow Chemical's intention to acquire it. That it was followed by no apparent response from regulators probably surprised no one. Observers may simply have ascribed that instance to the character of the Cox SEC and seen it as business as usual. Regulation in the Bush years appeared to many as an effort to discredit regulation itself, and to protect big players from any threat posed by other participants. That is certainly how I saw it.

All the campaign rhetoric notwithstanding, this mode of regulation continues in 2009. Back to Rohm and Haas. After the initial deal announcement, that stock went into a long, dark tunnel of uncertainty—and litigation—about whether and at what price there would be a closing. Finally, in early 2009, the shares settled down at a price that reflected all available public information. For months, it traded two to three million shares a day, at a price in the fifties. It closed on Thursday, March 5 at fifty-four.

On Friday, March 6, it gained ten points to reach sixty-four, on 13.3 million shares traded. On Monday, March 9, it did the same again, gaining another ten, to reach seventy-four, on another 13.3 million shares traded. After the close on Monday, the announcement finally came, to the effect that the stock was now worth seventy-nine. So, there were two full trading days during which inside information made a few people an awful lot of money.

Actually, it is worse than that. If you are an individual investor trading through your retail broker, you might have a problem if you saw the stock moving on March 6 or 9 and bought it, even if you did so innocently. The firm's compliance officer might ask your broker about the trade, and he or she might bust it, depending on your answer. To participate safely in insider trading you have to be big.

It is beyond discouraging to believe that the SEC of 2009 is no different from that of 2008. On March 31, 2009, I sent an e-mail describing the Rohm and Haas situation to "enforcement@sec. gov" and got no response, not even an acknowledgment of receipt. On May 29, I sent another e-mail, with the subject line "following up to see if anyone is there". I said that it was important for the

SEC to look at this matter, if there was "ever to be an end to this appalling post-regulatory environment". Again, crickets.

Finally, on July 20, I wrote by snail mail to Robert Khuzami, Director of Enforcement at the SEC, Washington DC. I thought I might get some response this time when I added, "This is your chance to show everyone there is a new sheriff in town, one that believes regulations should either be enforced, or dropped altogether. I believe that Goldman Sachs was the only investment banker on the Dow Chemical/Rohm and Haas deal. As such, you may get some obstruction to any investigation of insider trading. So, this will be a test of whether that firm really is in charge of our country."

As of this writing, I still have heard nothing back. Maybe something is being done about all this, but it seems unlikely.

Reinhold Niehbur (*Moral Man and Immoral Society*, 1932) said, "Laissez-faire economic theory is maintained through the ignorant belief that the general welfare is best served by placing the least possible political restraints upon economic activity." He continued, "Its survival is due to the ignorance of those who suffer injustice from the application of this theory, but fail to attribute their difficulties to the social anarchy and political irresponsibility which the theory sanctions." In other words, today's deregulation is not what it pretends to be but is actually a form of regulation by those in control. It owes its success to the unusually high level of ignorance we seem to have achieved.

A good way to torpedo the whole idea of regulation is to put really bad people in charge of it. The Bush era "Brownie" at SEC was Christopher Cox. Worse is the Obama team's pick to replace him, Mary Schapiro. Before her appointment, she had been head of the National Association of Securities Dealers (NASD), which merged in 2007 with the New York Stock Exchange's regulatory arm to become FINRA. At these posts, Ms. Schapiro was more known for doing well than for doing good. During her tenure, years marked by unprecedented mayhem on Wall Street, NASD/FINRA's regulation of the broker dealers could most charitably be described as negligent. For her troubles, Ms. Schapiro's compensation, no doubt "performance-based", was $1.9 million at NASD in 2006. In 2007, after the merger to form FINRA, it jumped to a more appropriate $3 million.

Those of us who owned member firms at the time believe the issues go well beyond just incompetence and overcompensation. A part of the NASD/NYSE merger to form FINRA was a capital distribution to NASD members. NASD's equity at the time was, as I recall it, $1.4 billion, or $280,000 per member firm among 5,000 members. To get member approval for the merger, members were told that, after closing, there would be a distribution of $175 million, or $35,000 per firm, which in fact happened.

Members knew at the time that we were being fleeced. But NASD claimed there was an IRS ruling that placed a hard $35,000 cap on the distributions. It also said the IRS document was for some reason sealed, secret, and could not be disclosed. The proxy statement was obviously deceitful on this point, and an opposition effort was mounted, but NASD hired a proxy solicitation firm that counterlaunched its own aggressive process. Finally, on November 21, the merger was approved, although by only a 4 to 3 vote margin. There were just enough members concerned about risking $35,000 to put it over. In Wall Street parlance, they were picked off.

Regulatory agencies, ideally, should be about more than helping themselves, yet what happened here was clearly a grab. We know this because in March 2007, four months after the vote, the IRS said it had not limited the payment as NASD had said. In a private letter dated March 13, IRS said NASD could have paid a lot more than it did. Litigation against FINRA by two members (Benchmark Financial, Standard Investment) was begun and is still ongoing in U.S. District Court and Court of Appeals. It might go nowhere, on the grounds of regulatory immunity, but that outcome will only mean it was buried.

If Martha Stewart was supposed to go to prison, then so might Mary Schapiro. Instead, she is now the head of the SEC. No more needs to be said about the state of regulation today, or about how much change 2009 has brought. Really, criteria for selecting people should be more than that the allegations of wrongdoing against the candidate are as yet unproven. That is setting the bar too low.

This is the shape of the real Bernie Madoff scandal. He can be put in jail for 150 years or 1,000; it changes nothing. He is just a product, the inevitable creation of an environment of corruption and negligence, a kind of enforced laxity. In short, the regulators are no such thing. They are themselves just an extension of the stock market, an arm of it. They are encouraged in this behavior by media outlets that are also in thrall to, and committed to cheerleading, the stock market; who never tire of warning against letting regulation make the United States uncompetitive; who insist that the free market provides its own discipline; for whom the opposite of deregulation is always "overregulation". For this crowd, the Fed—yes, that Fed—should now be given more regulatory powers. Only in the Alice in Wonderland world of the stock market could such a thing be uttered with a straight face.

For twenty-plus years, the Fed has crushed the impulse to save, in order to minimize borrowing costs to Wall Street. It has said that asset bubbles cannot be identified and should not be prevented, but when they pop, they urgently need to be reflated with trillions of printed dollars. Its relentless negligence spawned whole new fields of money changing, conducted by what are generously called "financial institutions", whose growth is of value only to them. It forced the whole "securitization" machine to be invented, so lending could be financed in the absence of bank deposits. On top of all this, it neglected its primary function, which has less to do with interest rates or the money supply than with regulation, preventing what happened to the banking system from happening. It saw to it, for example, that reasonable capital ratios did not impede reckless borrowing.

In short, the Fed brought the house down. An institution cannot provide stability and order if it does not even concede the existence of instability and disorder, let alone induces them. Nominating the Fed as a regulator of anything is not a good idea, unless we want more chaos. Representative Ron Paul of Texas wants the General Accountability Office to do an audit of the Fed for Congress, delving into its secret bailouts, short-term loans, and securities-buying with printed money—i.e., all its efforts to benefit the people who helped the Fed make the mess. Naturally, Mr. Bernanke is opposed. In the most ironic position ever taken, he says this could lead to congressional policy involvement that would be "highly destructive to the stability of the financial system, the dollar, and our national economic situation" (House hearing, June 2009).

At this writing, there are some regulatory reform proposals being floated in Washington, as might be expected following so much destruction. But the one important reform would be to unrepeal Glass Steagall. By this one measure all the others become unnecessary; without it, they mean little. Perhaps for this reason, neither political party will even suggest it. This is not just because Wall Street is spending millions on lobbyists. It is also because, except for Paul Volcker, there is no one with any credibility, no one who is not himself or herself part of the problem, and Mr.

Volcker does not want the reform job. Probably he knows it would kill him.

So, nothing changes. This is bad—worse than before. The bubble has been blown back up, but that is all. Gambling with no risk and no oversight or controls, and lots of free money from the Fed, and the assurance of taxpayer rescue in the event of loss— that is the continuing situation. Big money has a strong sense of entitlement; it expects special treatment, and it is prepared to do what it takes to keep its special advantages. In August of 2007, Secretary Paulson said he did not believe in more regulation. "I don't think it's constructive right now in the middle of this market turmoil to start pointing fingers and making specific policy recommendations."

Of course, finger-pointing is exactly what should be happening right now. Mr. Paulson's statement is stunning. It goes beyond simply fatuous. It is a parable of the radical, conceited, stock market–obsessed negligence and deceit and corruption so characteristic of twenty-first-century America. Plus, as always, the supreme lack of accountability.

Which reminds me of Goldman Sachs, which in 2009 became everyone's punching bag. I wrote on the subject two years earlier in my company's monthly newsletter:

> *Finally, less regulation seems to us another bizarre prescription. When the history of this period is written, it will highlight*

the forces and impact of aggressive deregulation, not excessive regulation. The example that gets used will be Goldman Sachs. We (and, we discover, others) have wondered how that firm, now mainly engaged in betting the house money, does so much better than its clients do. Goldman Sachs' prop trading consistently outearns what efficient-market theorists say is possible.

Most people have been prepared to assume this is due to very talented people working very long hours, and we certainly imagine this is part of it. But if that were the only explanation, clients of Goldman Sachs hedge funds and mutual funds would equally be cleaning up, but they are not. Plainly, the firm is doing different things with its own money than with its clients' money. If we at our firm traded against or in front of our recommendations, we would be in a lot of trouble with NASD. Goldman Sachs, on the other hand, can be a huge hedge fund manager, mutual fund manager, IPO originator, keeper of the market-leading commodities index, and still put its real resources into proprietary trading.

The wonder about Wall Street today is that individuals and institutions alike keep paying their fees and commissions to firms that are no longer client-oriented, and that may be using client information. Wall Street is a wide open town, where the business model is based on conflict of interest. Less regulation in this environment would hardly be possible.

—March, 2007

I was inspired to write this because I became fascinated with how much better Goldman Sachs was doing with its own money than with its clients' money. The only way this could be happening is if it were doing things with its own money that it was not doing for its fee-paying clients, which is a working definition of conflict of interest. Later examples of this model that have come to light include selling and/or shorting the same bad securities it sells to the public, and using privileged information to trade for its own account, with its paying customers either not being so treated, or only very selectively. It is not surprising that people like John Thain, Bob Rubin, Jon Corzine, and Hank Paulson do so wonderfully well for themselves at Goldman Sachs, and then struggle when they step out of that hothouse environment.

The point here is not to bash Goldman Sachs, although that is certainly in order and years overdue. Instead, Goldman should be seen as a creature of deregulation—aggressive, prolonged, fevered deregulation. That is what needs to be changed, and then Goldman Sachs would just wither away.

On the regulatory side, we need to go back to 1933 and reinstall Glass Steagall, separating the deposit-taking activity from the casino, reversing the recent bank charters of nonbanks. Do you know anyone with a Goldman Sachs credit card, or an auto loan, small business loan, or mortgage from Goldman Sachs? For future trades, get rid of both mark-to-model and mark-to-market; carry everything at cost until it is sold. Then cash compensation gets paid out of cash profits, and the whole issue of clawbacks or not goes away. Stop scapegoating the rating agencies, which of course are conflicted and corrupt, but everyone knew it.

The SEC and Treasury should get new heads—people who are honest and pay their taxes. They will then be in a position to file the lawsuits and launch criminal investigations of fraud and racketeering. This cannot happen until we replace all the regulatory hacks and shills at the top with professionals who are clean and who actually believe in regulation, not as a stepping-stone to riches for themselves, but as an end in itself. Give these people a lot more resources. Appoint Sheila Bair, head of FDIC, as Fed chair, and let her oversee the breakup of all the banks that are too big to fail. Drop the notion that something bad is no longer bad if it is disclosed.

Call all this witch-hunting or populism or blame game or finger-pointing or politics. It is actually accountability; it is simple justice, and it is long-past time for some. Investigations and penalties, regulation and enforcement, these are the essentials of trust and belief in the system. Sadly, none of this will happen, or even be proposed, for fear of upsetting the stock market. Now that we have installed a stock market–centric economy, not upsetting it becomes the prime directive. In the meantime, in 2009, the financial industry spent $38 million per month lobbying on Capitol Hill to make sure nothing changes. The forces of change cannot compete with this.

Lie 6.

Bailing out Wall Street Was Necessary to Preserve the System.

Fifty years ago, Connie Francis asked Neil Sedaka to write a song for her, on a rush basis. It had to be over the weekend, for a movie she was making about Fort Lauderdale over spring break. In three days, he wrote "Where the Boys Are". It was a masterpiece.

So, good things can be done under pressure, on a rush basis (Gettysburg Address, Hallelujah Chorus). The Wall Street bailout of 2008–2009 was not such a case. It turned out much less well than "Where the Boys Are". It is why the Obama administration was impaired and losing approval in less than a year. It was its war in Iraq, that thing that is so wrong, such a constellation of lies, from which there is no easy way back, no quick regaining of credibility. Saying that we would have been worse off without it is like saying the war in Iraq is why the terrorists have not hit us again—very clever, but a lie. Even the banks have said they were never really in distress, and they certainly did nothing to pass the bailout money along. So, just in this one decade, we have witnessed two of the most shameful miscarriages in American history. The first one banished forever our standing as a nonaggressor; the second, our pretenses about free-market capitalism.

The Wall Street bailout also banished our pose about fair play. For many generations, Americans found a way to tolerate Wall Street, showing a kind of philosophical resignation about it and believing in its centrality to capitalism. But then the financial sector became net extractive to the system (see Lie 3). Still, it was tolerated, but only until it needed bailing out. That Wall Street persistently extracted resources from the economy was bad enough, but that the public now directed taxpayer resources to it is too much. Real capitalism would have meant letting creditors, "trading partners", and shareholders take the whole hit, but this was not allowed to happen. The discipline of the market was rejected.

As such, the problems are all far worse now than they were before, just as they are with the war on terror. The whole effort has been to restore the *ex-ante* situation, to recreate what all have decried. In just two years, the new Federal debt equals all the debt accumulated previously. The money funneled to Wall Street, variously estimated at $2–$3 trillion, could have covered the nation's total health care bill, as staggering as that is, for a year. In other words, the Wall Street bailout does not just have bad aesthetics or bad moral values; it is crowding out worthwhile efforts.

The Wall Street bailout also banished the pose about America being a representative, democratic place. The people did not want it. This was one time—an extremely important time—when some Republicans got it right and voted no. A huge majority of those polled who wrote or called their elected representatives were opposed to the bailout, but it passed anyway. Our government then refused even to disclose where the money went, claiming that would undermine confidence.

It is significant that Democrats, although they did not invent it, forced the bailout on America, with most Republicans in Congress opposed. This ended the honeymoon we were otherwise ready to have with the new administration and Congress. It made Harry Reid and Nancy Pelosi into villains, and it renewed Sarah Palin. All this happened because Washington was finally, conclusively, revealed as a tool of Wall Street and an enemy of the people. Ron Paul, Ralph Nader, Bernie Sanders, and Ross Perot were right all along, however much they were marginalized and ridiculed.

Jobs have been lost, and retirement savings. Homes have been foreclosed on, plants shut down, and small businesses closed. In response, Congress, the Fed, and Treasury all mobilized to help out the people who caused it. The explosion in money supply has bypassed goods and services purchases and gone straight to financial markets. There, it has reflated the bubble, revived speculation, and restored bonuses. The exercise never had anything to do with the real economy, or it would have simply guaranteed deposits, not the institutions, which should have been allowed to fail. And the cost truly challenges the imagination—so far, almost $10,000 for every American man, woman, and child. This is not free-market capitalism, but reverse socialism, a wealth transfer from the public to private ownership, and a massive redistribution upward. Quantitative easing, for example, is the use of public funds to purchase private securities—not to hold them, but to relieve the sellers until they can buy them back.

The public is making big sacrifices on behalf of the creators and enablers of the ghastly mess. Neither the U.S. government nor the relevant agencies have any allegiance to, or interest in, taxpayers or the investing public. Their only fealty is to the financiers who have bought and paid for the present system. There is just no other way to explain what happens at AIG or Citigroup. Very big decisions get made on weekends at hurry-up meetings. The clear priority is not doing what is right or makes sense, but doing it before the market opens on Monday. Our top-down obsession with the stock market and all its short-term fluctuations has reduced America to a very silly state, involved more than anything else in trying to please the very people who have ruined it for everyone.

How do we know the bailout was not to save the real economy? For one thing, it never did increase bank lending. In this regard, it is important to recognize the mutation banks have undergone. Even to call them banks is at best imprecise. The twenty-first-century big bank stopped being primarily a source of loans or an allocator of capital. Instead, it became a hedge fund (just as the hedge funds became lenders). The real action was proprietary trading, betting the house money for its own benefit, with shareholders and depositors providing the table stakes, leveraged by a stack of cheap money from the Fed. Shareholders got half the winnings, which we now know were bogus, after the players took half for themselves, cash bonuses paid out of noncash profits. Financial author Michael Lewis calls this fraud.

Another indicator of corruption is complexity. An honest plan is simple and direct. The Wall Street bailout was complex and obscure, usually undisclosed. For example, it suggests that A lends to B, who will transact with C, who might then lend to D. It is like the Rube Goldberg machine, where a ball rolls down an incline, drops into a shovel, which tips it into a spiral, where it goes around and around, etc. The analogy breaks down, though, because in Rube Goldberg's creations, causation was inviolate. His creations were elaborate but functional. In the TARP (Troubled Asset Relief Program) world, causation breaks down before the stated objective of inducing new lending is achieved.

We have seen this kind of policy by indirection before. It was not important to catch Osama, who actually did 9/11; he was marginal. Instead, we had to invade Iraq, which had nothing to do with 9/11, because that would cause a change in the region, which would induce a behavior change elsewhere. Likewise with trickle-down:— if we cut taxes on rich people, it will induce them to behaviors that will have the effect of creating jobs. Neither of these cons, we now know, had any merit or honesty. Rube Goldberg would have scoffed at them. But they were vigorously put forward, very forcefully asserted, and America went along. So it was with the bank bailout. The program had nothing to do with stimulating lending.

TARP (Targeted At Rich People) was just an enormous wealth transfer from the public to big money, with no strings attached, not even disclosure of where the money went. It went to cover bad side bets, to pay off "counterparties", in a pointless roulette called derivatives trading, having nothing whatever to do with capitalism or the economy. At AIG, for example, the bailout money went to meet collateral calls from other gamblers, most prominently Goldman Sachs. There is no excuse for TARP, which is why it seems so complicated, and why where the money went was concealed for so long. It was just a scheme for protecting big money from the consequences of its own mistakes.

Years ago, U.S. citizens allowed their national public servants to take huge campaign contributions, and Wall Street had money to contribute. Big money wanted tax cuts for itself; it wanted deregulation of everything; it wanted a low short-term interest rate. Politicians were paid a lot of money to oblige. Then, big money wanted TARP, and the government had to figure out how to channel trillions more dollars to it while telling the public it was to save the system. Actually, the only way to save the system was to let the free market sort it out, not socialize the loss. Guarantee the deposits and fund the lending, set up "good banks", protect the payment system, but let the toxic assets and their holders take their own hit.

In the emergency of the early 1930s, FDR declared bank holidays. By the time the banks reopened, the public knew which ones were sound. He passed the 1934 regulations forbidding deposit-taking banks from betting in the stock market, and he signed FDIC into law. The direct cost to the government of all this was zero, and it worked. What is different between then and now? Then, it was not part of the national agenda to serve and protect the people at the top. Today, that is the whole agenda.

The stock-market economy that America is trapped in is now perfectly corrupt. Some very big people at the top have arranged things so they will get bigger and bigger. The way this all gets financed is that other people have to take a very big hit. Investors and taxpayers and employees are the saps at the table. There can be no more vivid illustration of this than the China Syndrome called AIG, in which we see a direct transfer of wealth from the public to the people who made the mess, to be distributed at their sole discretion.

So far, however, Congress can only think in twelve-figure amounts. For really colossal malfeasance today, you have to think in thirteen figures. And for this, you need our old friend, the "independent" (answers only to the banks) Federal Reserve. First, in December 2008, the Fed cut the overnight funds rate basically to zero, but no one expected any effect from this on the real economy (see Lie 2), and there was none. The lack of response gave the Fed cover to do what it really wanted to do, which was quantitative easing.

Quantitative easing is printing new dollars out of the ether from the Fed's toolbox and using them to reflate financial asset prices. This process is called growing the Fed's balance sheet, which, at this writing, is over $2 trillion. The Fed does this by becoming the big, new buyer in the market for existing securities. Naturally, its purchases are kept secret from the public; only the sellers know what is happening.

I should stop here to remark on something important about governance. As nearly as I can determine, the Federal Reserve should serve Congress and answer to it, not to the executive branch—certainly not to Wall Street. It is supposed to get its power from Congress; it is simply false to claim that the Fed should be "independent" from it. Yet years of watching CNBC and reading the *Wall Street Journal* (I do neither) have persuaded America of something curious—namely, that the Fed answers only to itself; that if it were answerable to Congress, it would become politicized; and that when the chairman makes what are mandated appearances before Congress, he is really just making a sort of courtesy call.

This modern conception of the Fed, which has taken deep root, is quite dangerous. It enables the Fed to rescue Wall Street—not the banking system, but the shareholders and management. This, it was never empowered to do; it just did it. If the executive branch or the legislative branch wanted to do this, it should have been up to them to implement what was essentially a fiscal policy move. Instead, we got a lot of behind-closed-doors activity, some of which may have been illegal under the Federal Reserve Act, or unconstitutional, or both, and which damaged Americans' trust in their government.

As the Fed "balance sheet" goes up in trillions, so do financial asset prices. That is the bookkeeping. The pose has been that the Fed's purchasing is in mortgage-related securities, for which it has budgeted $1.25 trillion (plus another $200 billion for Treasuries), so that the effect will be lower borrowing costs for homebuyers. The Fed now buys virtually all (at least 80 percent) new mortgage securities, becoming in effect the lender for today's housing market. It does this by creating trillions of dollars out of thin air and buying repackaged loans above the market, on which it will take big losses when it sells.

The main impact of quantitative easing, however, has not been on housing activity, which remains as moribund as the rest of the real economy, nor even on the holders of mortgage-backed securities. One or more of the two hundred PhD researchers on staff at the Federal Reserve should have foreseen what would happen. We know that fiddling with the Fed funds rate does little to affect the rates at which people actually borrow (mortgage, car loan, credit card); it just raises the net interest margin to banks. That is why the use of the plural when talking about Fed lowering or raising of interest rates is such a deceit. But what about quantitative easing?

Quantitative easing is like going down to the lake with a fire hose, and saying you plan to raise just the south end of the lake. It does not take Archimedes to realize that is an unpromising enterprise. It does not take two hundred PhDs to understand that quantitative easing will not work, either. Markets exist to arbitrage it away. "Traders" get paid ungodly amounts to sit in front of screens, watch for market distortions, and instantly erase them.

The practical consequence of the Fed's actions, as of this writing, has been an astonishingly strong and rapid reflation of financial asset prices, across the board. This is what the Fed has done for over twenty years—inflate and reflate, inflate and reflate financial assets. That is all it does, but it certainly does that. Since quantitative easing began in early 2009, there have been unbelievable rallies in stocks, bonds, commodities, precious metals, foreign currencies, you name it. Any dispassionate analysis must conclude that prices now far exceed values. To me, the most remarkable case may be corporate fixed income, especially high-yield debt, where yield premiums have all but vanished. Even companies known to be weak credits can now issue long-term bonds at yields below what Treasuries would pay, if it were not for quantitative easing.

Sometime in 2010 quantitative easing will end and with it, the rally in bonds. The "trade" then will be to reallocate out of bonds into stocks, giving the latter another big boost. So, the only effect of all the Fed's exertions (and I believe its only intention) will have been a reflation of the stock market.

Concurrently, back in the real world, home prices have not recovered at all, and foreclosures mount; job losses continue; auto sales are still down by 40 percent; small businesses keep closing; plants are still shutting down; big business keeps laying off and cutting and closing. Mortgage applications in late 2009 were at the lowest level since 1997.

There are just two possible explanations for this set of outcomes. One, the Fed and all its brainiacs are just incompetent. Two, it was never their intention to do more than save Wall Street. Both Mr. Greenspan and Mr. Bernanke are, after all, a couple of Republicans for whom unemployment is just an abstraction, and seeking full employment is just something to tell Congress you are committed to doing.

It is the same as with TARP. There, banks are frantic to repay, and the government is letting them, before there has been any increase in lending. The conclusion is unavoidable. The programs are either incompetent or they never had anything to do with the real economy. Four possible uses of the money were: a) boost capital; b) increase lending; c) repay it; and d) boost executive compensation. Which happened? There was never any doubt: c and d.

On the matter of paying the money back, let's stop the cheering. If I am tied, hand and foot, to the railroad track, and the train is rumbling down the track straight for me, I really need a rescue. If you then come along and stop, get out of your car, and untie me, right before the train roars past, you have rescued me. Great. Let's say then that I hand you $100 to reimburse you for your time and trouble. You might be whole, but we are not even up; we are not all square. I will go on owing you, big-time, for the rest of my life. I can never repay you.

Is this too harsh? Not necessarily. By buying securities from the banks, the Fed increased their reserves. The increased reserves could have backed greater lending, but they did not. Instead, excess reserves simply accumulated, approaching $1 trillion. Not only that, the Fed has, at this writing, a plan to prevent growth in lending, using a new authority it has given itself, by paying interest to banks on their reserves. By making it more attractive for banks to keep reserves on deposit, the Fed plans to keep those funds at the banks, so they are available to use to buy securities back from it later. So, from start to finish, the whole exercise had nothing to do with extending more credit to the real economy.

Government assistance to Wall Street goes beyond even direct "investments" and quantitative easing. There are big, new credit lines from the Fed; guarantees of bad assets held by banks; guarantees of $300 billion in debt issued by banks; plus, the invaluable message conveyed to the world that America has no priority higher than serving its money men, that its full faith and credit stand behind them. Under something called the Temporary Liquidity Guarantee Program, over $300 billion of corporate debt was issued, by October 2009, with a government guarantee. That is, taxpayers explicitly backed new private debt they knew nothing about. Under this particular bailout vehicle, GE, that rock-ribbed paragon of American capitalism, issued $60 billion.

Between TARP (relatively small), Federal guarantees, and Fed money creation, the commitment might come to several trillion dollars. In addition, in 2009, the industry got Congress to lean on the Financial Accounting Standards Board, which voted (3 to 2) to relax its fair market value reporting rules. This relaxation allowed firms to use their own judgment about when to book losses on bad assets. Basically, this rule change allows firms to report fake profits. The only thing not fake is the bonuses paid from those profits.

The record size of Wall Street's profits and bonuses in 2009 has been well reported. It is surprising that they have not been higher. After all, it was only necessary to keep the money for in-house "trading" and take a long position in anything financial. The town simpleton would have known this much, let alone all our high-finance types. Then, leverage the position ten to one, using the free money made available to banks by the Fed; nothing enhances returns like borrowing at zero. Between quantitative easing and no-cost credit, the "independent" Fed made at least a double gift to Wall Street. Everyone else can go pound sand, but at least we restored the money changers, and God bless America.

Finance today is parasitic, destructive, useless, and dangerous, and so are government actions that support it. No one has a Goldman Sachs credit card, or an auto loan, mortgage, small business loan, or big business credit line from Goldman Sachs. That firm's only connection with the real economy is as a drain on it, or as an arranger of transactions that produce only layoffs. It is too bad that our highest national priority, to which we devote unlimited, undisclosed, and unhesitating resources, is to serve it.

Lie 7.

The Health Care Question Is about Who Pays.

The theme of this book is that it is in the nature of things that great concentrations of wealth produce sufficient power to corrupt. This is not an original thought. As Reinhold Niebuhr says, such power will do what is necessary to perpetuate itself. It is not just the world of finance that is susceptible. It is much broader than that. This chapter is only one illustration. It is about corn. As such, it may seem like a departure, but it is intended to be of a piece.

The health care question is, of course, partly about who pays for it. But this is not the whole subject, or even the most important part of it. The really interesting question is not who should pay, but why it costs so much.

By now, we are all drearily aware of the huge amounts America spends on health care. It is now running at $1 out of every $6 in the economy—over $2.3 trillion in 2008, and growing. This was $7,700 for each man, woman, and child. As health care consumes more national resources, it increasingly crowds out other useful activities, producing an increasingly stressed society. The popular assumption has been that this is simply due to an inefficient delivery system, one laced with perverse incentives, bureaucracy, redundancies, and layering of all sorts, not to mention venality and corruption.

No doubt, these factors are present, although I think they may be overdrawn. My own firsthand experience with the health care system, thankfully limited so far, has been quite positive. The care itself was fantastic, almost unnaturally professional on the part of both doctors and nurses. (These people should almost be better rewarded in a society that showers riches on others who contribute so little.) The administrative aspects, as I recall, were not especially onerous or inefficient. The expense was obvious— the rooms with motorized beds and monitors on the wall, the medications, tests, labs, and staffing. I did not, however, observe or experience particular incidences of over recommending tests or procedures or medications, certainly nothing to compare with the over recommending found on Wall Street.

Also, if it were just a matter of inefficiency, the outcomes would be better. It would be expensive, but at least we would be healthier than we are, not less healthy than the people in other highly developed countries. This is what the U.S. health care debate is missing—the causes of the poor U.S. health itself. It is the thesis here that a big cause is our underlying poor diet—specifically, our uniquely corn-based diet. The corn-driven American diet is acting like a slow poison, with which a huge portion of U.S. health care is trying to contend.

By one estimate, the United States now spends $500 billion a year, or 3–4 percent of GDP, on preventable, diet-linked, chronic diseases, all traceable to our being overweight. Actually, the Center for Disease Control puts it higher than this: it says that three-quarters of our health care spending, or over $1.7 trillion, is for such preventable, chronic diseases. Split the difference, and call it $1.1 trillion—half the health care tab—for obesity, diabetes, heart disease, and cancers linked to diet. And it keeps growing. If current trends continue, 103 million Americans will be obese in 2018, or 43 percent of adults, compared with 31 percent in 2008 (Emory University research). Obesity, meanwhile, is a known promoter of diabetes and hypertension. The author of this study, Kenneth E. Thorpe, an authority on the cost of treating chronic disease, says, "If we're interested in bending the cost curve, we've got to go back to the source of what's driving spending. It's the explosion of chronic disease."

Corn has just one use or outcome, in animals and in humans— namely, the production of fat. We might drastically cut our health care costs by getting the massive amounts of corn out of the American food supply. Corn's only dietary uses are in fattening up livestock or in being milled into junk food or processed into corn fructose. As such, its contributions, uniquely American, are heart disease, obesity, and diabetes. One way to reduce corn content would be to put a dedicated health care tax on corn-containing meat, processed foods, and fructose-sweetened soda pop. At a bare minimum, we could stop using taxpayer money to subsidize the growing of corn.

Grower subsidies have been a sore point for years. The farm bill is a transfer payment to growers, an entitlement. It typically does not even go to the operators, the ones riding in tractor cabs, but to absentee landlords living in New York and Beverly Hills. As the legislation makes its way through Congress, it picks up more and more unrelated amendments to buy off critics, some of which are actually good (food stamps, school lunch) but are making it more and more expensive. Meanwhile, the commodity title survives, with no caps or even a pretense of being downside protection, even when crop prices and farm income are through the roof.

These transfer payments have had a profound effect on industry practices. The subsidies have made corn a huge phenomenon it would not otherwise be. Federal payments made this crop so ubiquitous by stimulating production and, until very recently, letting the grain be bought for less than the cost of growing it. Before fuel ethanol came along, corn was made artificially cheap by taxpayer support. This economic distortion in turn drove down the prices of foods that could incorporate corn, thus substituting processed food for unprocessed.

The corn industrial complex likes to boast about how affordable it has made getting calories, which is commendable up to a point. But what it also means is that we eat hundreds, maybe thousands, more calories per day than we need, or than non-Americans do. This in turn means that we weigh more and more, two-thirds of us being overweight and half of those obese. In turn, this means one in three of us born in 2000 will get type 2 diabetes. Combined with heart disease, these effects mean that for the first time in our history, American life expectancy is getting shorter. Four of our top ten killers are largely the result of diet. Michael Pollan says, "The health care crisis is a euphemism for problems induced by the American diet." We subsidize all this mayhem by subsidizing corn, and with it the cheap calories from hydrogenated corn oil and high fructose corn syrup.

Subsidized grain also means animals being fed corn at feedlots that can buy it cheaply, below grower cost, so beef cattle, poultry, swine, and dairy cows can all be fattened at animal feedlots, instead of on range and pasture grasses. This factory feeding produces animals diseased by fecal bacteria and deprived of all manner of nutrition, but these problems have been addressed by a big animal antibiotic and vitamin industry.

Corn-growing itself is not the only subsidy beneficiary—there is also corn-refining. Sugar import tariffs have for decades supported an otherwise uneconomic market for high fructose corn syrup. HFCS is used in pastries and baked goods, ketchup, jams and jellies, syrup, and candy, but most of all in sodas. When it comes to effective lobbying, Archer Daniels Midland taught the pharmaceutical companies, the oil companies, and the insurance lobby everything they know.

So, what is it about corn? Sweet corn, the kind people eat, is not a particularly good food. It is high-starch, glycemic, empty calories compared to green vegetables. Milled corn becomes junk food and corn fructose, leading causes of diabetes and obesity. About 10 percent of American calorie intake comes from corn fructose alone.

Feed grain corn is used to fatten up U.S. beef, swine, and poultry, making American meat a uniquely high-risk food, promoting heart disease and cancers compared to meat from grass-fed animals. A corn-based animal diet, versus grass-fed, elevates saturated fats and triglycerides and lowers antioxidants.

The literature is extensive and growing on the health effects of a corn-driven diet. A sampling of findings follows.

As I have mentioned, about 10 percent of American calories comes just from corn fructose. The contribution of corn fructose to obesity and diabetes is generally agreed to be higher today than this. The reason for this disproportionate contribution is not just that the sweetener's relatively low cost encourages overconsumption of beverages and foods that contain it. (This has been the Corn Refiners Association argument.) Obesity is partly a function not just of caloric intake, but of the calorie sources. The body makes fat faster from fructose than from glucose (the two sugars; sucrose is a bonded fructose and glucose). Specifically, fructose gets processed by the liver to fatty acids faster than glucose does; it makes triglyceride faster.

It is generally agreed that obesity may be related (in a causal way) to diabetes, which would help explain why America is seeing an epidemic of both. Diabetes (type 2, specifically) is high blood sugar, and obesity increases insulin resistance. A diet high in refined products is especially conducive to high blood sugar. In addition, soda with HFCS is rich in reactive carbonyl compounds, which are elevated in diabetics and cause complications.

The most disturbing studies, however, concern the nutritional content of the meat and dairy products that come from grain-fed (corn) cattle, swine, and poultry.

Beef cattle were evolved to eat grass; a corn diet hurts their digestive system, which makes it necessary to give them antibiotics to control infections. More important, meat from grass-fed animals is lower in total fat and higher in several antioxidants than meat from grain-fed animals. Grass-fed cows produce butter that has less saturated fat and more CLA, vitamin E, beta carotene, and omega-3 fatty acids. The meat and eggs from chickens raised indoors on corn and deprived of greens are low in nutrients. Eggs from pastured chickens contain one-third less cholesterol; one-quarter less saturated fat; two times more omega-3s; seven times more beta carotene; and two-thirds more vitamin A.

Grass is rich in such antioxidant vitamins as beta carotene and vitamin E, so depriving animals of grass is depriving them of nutrients. Food color is sometimes an indication. In healthy meat, for example, beta carotene gives a creamy color to the fat which is absent in the fat of grain-fed animals. In eggs, the more orange the yolk, the healthier; yolks from pastured poultry eggs are vivid. Three nutrients are especially important here:

Vitamin E levels are much higher in grass than in grain. Vitamin E deficiencies in humans have been linked by one study or another with diabetes, immune disorders and AIDS, Parkinson's, eye disease, lung and liver diseases, heart disease, and cancer. Compared with grain-fed, pigs have four times the vitamin E in their milk when raised on pasture. Grass-fed beef has meat four times higher in vitamin E than grain-fed, and even two times higher than with vitamin E added to grain-fed. An egg from a pastured hen has 30 percent more vitamin E, even compared with hens on grain feed that is supplemented.

Conjugated linoleic acid (CLA) reduces both cancer risk and tumor growth and is one of the most potent anticancer agents. Grass-fed animals produce meat and dairy products containing three to five times more CLA than do grain-fed animals. The cheese from grass-fed dairy cows has more than four times the CLA of cheese from feedlot cows. The milk from grass-fed Irish cows is two to three times higher in CLA than from grain-fed American cows. Raising dairy cows on fresh pasture versus giving them standard feed increases CLA in milk by five times.

Omega-3 fatty acids reduce risk of cancer, cardiovascular disease, allergies, depression, obesity, and autoimmune disorders. Grain-fed beef is not only artificially high in total fat and low in vitamin E, beta carotene, and CLA, it is also low in omega-3s. A ratio of omega-6s to Omega 3s of four or lower is considered ideal, and in grass-fed beef it is 2:1. In grain-fed beef, it is over 14:1. Eggs from pastured hens have two to twenty times more omega-3s, and the meat, two to four times more, than from grain-fed hens.

Our health care crisis in this country will be solved not by shifting the costs around but by cutting them. Public policy will be forced one day to address the bizarre contradiction between using precious public resources to produce something harmful and then using more resources to address the harm.

The corn-driven American diet is acting like a slow poison on us, and we are subsidizing it with huge transfer payments and then treating the results at huge expense. With a lot of education, this will become better known, producing a profound change in consumer habits long before any change is permitted in public policy. It will come from the bottom up. The corn industrial complex has a hold on our government that makes other lobbies look like amateurs.

I have thought that change would take a very long time, given the force of the corn industrial complex. But in September 2009, Michael Pollan did a column in the *New York Times* that was a tour de force, arguing that health care reform legislation might unintentionally hasten change.

Pollan's thesis is that any version of reform will bring change. At present, health insurers control claims through coverage caps or with rules against preexisting conditions or other techniques for keeping at-risk patients out of the customer pool, thus limiting their exposure to the chronic diseases that come from a corn-based diet.

Pollan points out that even modest, privatized reform calls for ending these techniques and instead keeping customers enrolled, regardless of health. This will bring a sea change in insurers' attitudes toward bad health, which they will now oppose, as their old way of controlling claims is eliminated. Reform will, even if inadvertently, introduce into the system an impulse to care about bad health. Thus the corn industry will have a big new opponent that will start buying its own seats on congressional ag committees.

Corn is what is wrong with America. It is why our health is so poor relative to what we spend on health care. More important, it tracks us on the iron rails of corruption. It demands to be subsidized; it insists. In all the coverage of the Iowa caucuses, it is never mentioned that candidates from both parties must pledge allegiance to the protection racket of corn if they are to have any chance. Since Iowa is the first state to pick candidates, what they all learn is that in America, the first step is to sell your soul.

AFTERWORD

A lot happened in early 2010. The jobs picture kept on worsening. Aside from chanting the word, nothing is in prospect to change it. What still rings the dinner bell for the CEO class is layoffs, lots of them. Until this dynamic changes, little tax schemes will be just more corporate welfare, while public sector programs get derided.

The White House has elevated Mr. Volcker over the creeps it was listening to before, and some regulatory reforms have been proposed, but Wall Street should have no difficulty swatting these away. Its latest pitch is that the Volcker Rule (separating proprietary betting from customer-related activity) is wrong because, "Gee, we only do a little of that bad proprietary stuff, and it did not cause the problem." In other words, the apocalyptic losses came through Wall Street's serving its clients. This statement is absurd even for Wall Street, but it is being aggressively put forward and seriously listened to. Then there are the veiled threats about lending being impaired, as if it were not already stalled. Not since the Bronze Age has there been a bunch with more brass than these people.

The 2008 crisis was caused by banks incurring big losses on their securities positions. These losses were so enormous they destabilized the banks (or their counterparties), which in turn threatened their lending activity, and thereby the credit system and the real economy. The one obvious, necessary, and sufficient way to prevent a recurrence is to disallow securities transactions (proprietary trading, owning hedge funds, underwriting) by federally backed lenders, and vice versa. In other words, reinstate Glass-Steagall, which kept the peace for six or seven decades after 1933, before its 1999 repeal. (After its repeal, the markets fell into chaos.)

During the bill-writing process in the Senate, an amendment that would un-repeal Glass-Steagall was proposed but not voted on. To separate banking from betting now, the best we can hope for is a strong version of the Volcker Rule, which would restrict banks from proprietary investing, that is, activity not related to serving clients. The trick will be in not allowing everything to be called client-related. The old, pre-1999 way, forcing banks to choose, whether they wanted to be fish or fowl, was better.

The Swiss have reversed themselves and decided not to give Treasury any UBS client information after all.

The Senate voted seventy to thirty to support Mr. Bernanke's reappointment, so as not to threaten the confidence of financial markets, in the biggest miscarriage since O. J. The vote drives another stout nail into the coffin of accountability. That is a loss. Accountability had a kind of biblical rightness to it.

The Supreme Court voted five to four to lift the heavy boot of oppression from the neck of big money, to restore to it the influence it has been so sorely lacking, by permitting even more of it to go to political campaigns.

In April 2010, BP's Deepwater Horizon oil rig blew out. This was a perfect example of what this book is about. That is, a government that has been bought with contributions from big-moneyed corporate interests; an industry-financed regulatory regime, in this case the Minerals Management Service, that amounts to self-regulation; and the relative lack of change brought by a change in Presidents. All of it being supported by a big lie, in this case, the one that says the way to deal with our dependence on oil is to increase our supply of it. When disaster struck, more lies came, to the effect that it was just a freak, unforeseeable occurrence, instead of the inevitable consequence of a fundamentally corrupt energy policy, plus numerous regulatory lapses.

An oil spill in the Gulf; financial reform that is not; Afghanistan policy that makes no sense to anyone; health care law that cements in place and expands the root cause of the problem. These are not random outcomes. They are the inevitable result of a system in thrall to the people with the fattest checkbooks, people who can grab the microphone and never let go because they will never have enough. (Mr. Obama's mistake was believing he should or could appease these people, which brought no change.)

The situation is nearly out of control. So, what should happen? A pessimist might say that not much will happen until it all gets worse. The history of nineteenth-century Russia under the czars is one of almost unbelievable popular forbearance for seven decades, so people do have a huge capacity to just go along before they say enough is enough. And most Americans can still go home and watch big-screen TVs.

On the other hand, America is an angry place today. Some people blame Obama and the Democrats; others, their predecessors. (The people who are really in charge must love this pointless feud.) America should be angry, and it is, so something may be coming.

There is really no prospect of resolving, or even seriously addressing, the individual issues raised in this book. Before that can happen, something more fundamental has to change—namely, the whole elaborate system of bribery and extortion that today forms the basis of our system of government. The enormous concentration of wealth must be separated from its undue influence, which means reforming campaign finance, lobbying, conglomerates owning the news, and think tanks. Free speech is a vital American value, and it is threatened today. Until this changes, we will go on getting wars and bailouts and bad health that nobody wanted.

The world is not fair, and it never will be. Fine, we get that. But some smart person, maybe JFK or maybe not, once said it is our task to hold two thoughts at the same time. They are in tension with each other, but we have to embrace them both. One, the world is not fair. Two, the direction of history, the point of it, is toward greater fairness. Some years from now, we will look back at today and ask, "What in the world was that? What were we all thinking?" We will see this time as a digression—an expensive one—from the path of our history.

Sources

The information herein has two sources, aside from the author's own experience and observation. First and foremost, the *New York Times*; second, Google Search, which was especially useful in connection with Lie 7. Here, sources included *Seeds of Deception; Eat Wild—Grass-Fed Food and Facts; Science Daily, Organic Food Directory.*

About the Author

Paul Christopherson was until 2008 chairman of New Vernon Associates, Inc., which he co-founded in 1992. New Vernon Associates was an institutional equity research firm. Paul was previously a longtime Wall Street analyst at Kidder, Peabody & Co., and Bear Stearns. A native of Minneapolis, he is also an ordained Episcopal priest.